The History & Treasures of
WINDSOR CASTLE
Robin Mackworth-Young

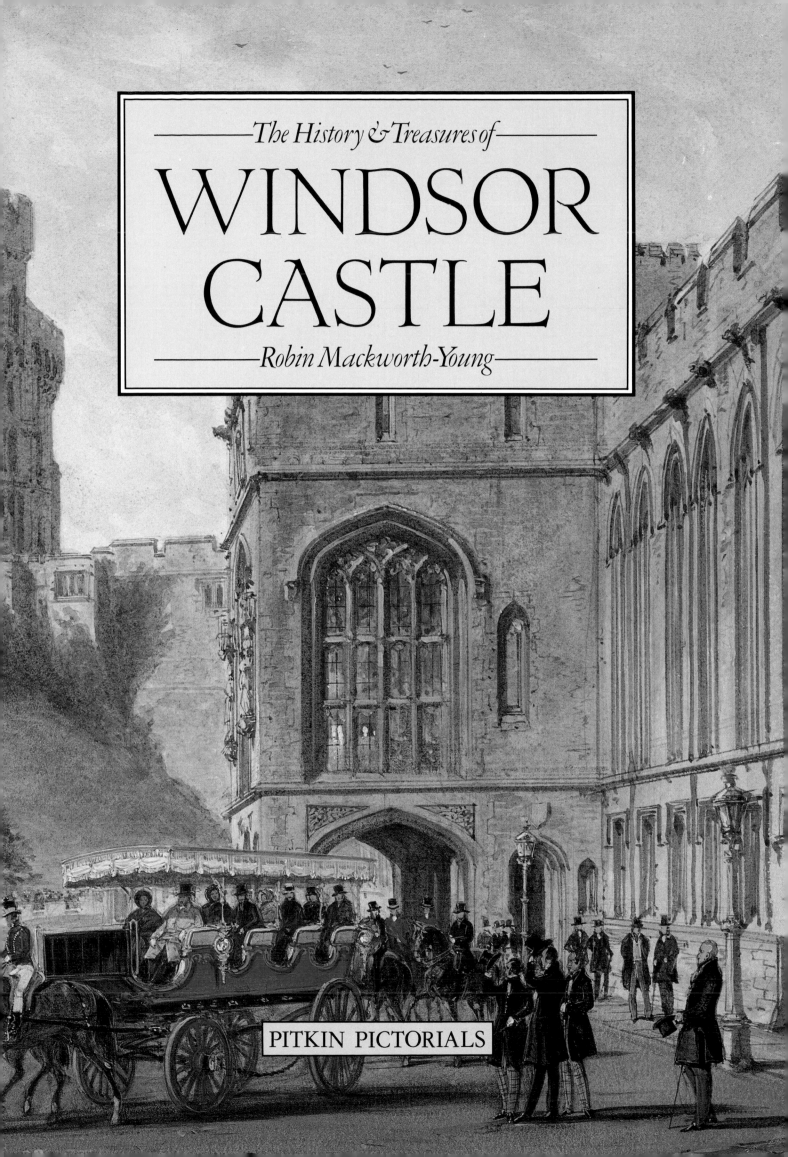

The History & Treasures of

WINDSOR CASTLE

Robin Mackworth-Young

PITKIN PICTORIALS

Author's Introduction

No book on Windsor Castle written since 1913 can fail to be based primarily on the monumental work of William St John Hope published in that year (*Windsor Castle, an Architectural History*). This inexhaustible quarry of information and learning does not, be it said, make for light bedtime reading. Nor does its author devote his attention with equal enthusiasm to all periods of the castle's life. His heart was in the Middle Ages, and interest wanes with succeeding centuries. This deficiency has been largely made good, though inevitably in less detail, by the sections on Windsor Castle in the later volumes of that exemplary publication *The History of the King's Works*, edited by Howard Colvin.

The architectural story of the castle is only one aspect of its history. Other books have appeared which lay greater emphasis on life in the castle, or on its place in the history of the nation. As to its contents, a vast and comprehensive series of *catalogues raisonnés*, begun 46 years ago with Lord Clark's catalogue of the drawings of Leonardo da Vinci, and now extending to works of art of all kinds in the royal residences, is in progress. Many have been, or are being, compiled by Sir Oliver Millar, Surveyor Emeritus of The Queen's Pictures, and Geoffrey de Bellaigue, Director of the Royal Collection and Surveyor of The Queen's Works of Art.

This book represents an attempt to draw all those threads together, and to trace the development of the castle from its beginnings as one of a series of spartan military outposts to a royal home as uniquely celebrated as the family to which it belongs. A volume of this size can naturally do no more than skim the surface. To take but one example: the works of art lodged in the castle include over 30,000 drawings, many of the finest quality. Only a fraction of these can even be mentioned, let alone illustrated. For any who wish to delve deeper, however, it may serve as an introduction to those more weighty volumes on which it is largely based.

There is one further purpose which this book aims to fulfil. It is the first on the castle as a whole in which the illustrations are as important as the text. This innovation calls for no apology. The astonishing advance in the techniques of colour reproduction has given a new dimension to the printed volume. Whatever the value of the written word in imparting information and ideas, there are some fields in which illustrations cannot fail to be more effective. 'Do not busy yourself with things belonging to the eyes', wrote that unsurpassed illustrator Leonardo da Vinci, 'by making them enter through the ears.' The two imaginative reconstructions of the castle in the early Middle Ages on pages 8 and 9, prepared expressly for this volume by Mr Terry Ball of the Inspectorate of Ancient Monuments, with the advice of two leading scholars in this field, tell us more in the space of a few square inches than could be conveyed by pages of elaborate prose. Nor could any book which included the treasures of the castle in its theme hope to give an adequate account without the help of the visual image.

Any work of this kind is in a sense the summation of the work of others, and it would be impossible even to determine, let alone recite here, the names of all whose labours have furnished raw material for its composition. One debt shall not, however, pass unrecorded. The delightful study of the castle by my late predecessor, Sir Owen Morshead, first published in 1951, is a continuing inspiration to all who work in this field. Less widely known are the considerable unpublished gleanings which he left behind him in the shape of numerous indexes and other compilations, whose usefulness is no less great, and no less lasting. To his name I would add those of my former colleagues Oliver Millar and Geoffrey de Bellaigue, without whose help and knowledge parts of this book could not have been written.

I leave to the last my weightiest obligation, which is to the owner of the castle and its contents. Not only does the copyright of most of the illustrations belong to The Queen, but no work of this kind would, or could, be undertaken without Her Majesty's gracious assent. For this I humbly record my deep and dutiful thanks.

The author, Sir Robin Mackworth-Young, GCVO, Librarian Emeritus, was Librarian at Windsor Castle and Assistant Keeper of The Queen's Archives from 1958 to 1985.

ABOVE: 'Saint George's Gateway, Edward III's Tower and Round Tower'. An engraving by W. Alfred Delamotte, 1844.

BELOW: Delamotte's engraving entitled 'Old Oak and Beech Tree in Windsor Forest', 1844.

ABOVE. Windsor Castle from St Leonard's Hill, 1839, by C. R. Stanley.

The Normans

Perhaps the largest fortress of its kind in the world, Windsor Castle has belonged continuously to the sovereigns of England since the days of the Norman Conquest over 900 years ago. It must be by far the oldest royal residence still in regular use today, and its present occupant, Her Majesty Queen Elizabeth II, is a direct descendant of its founder.

It was not as a stone-walled castle but as a stronghold of earth and timber that it first sprang into existence, one of many constructed by the forces of William the Conqueror to reduce and control the country after his invasion of 1066.

The Normans had evolved a unique kind of fortress, far stronger than anything known to the Anglo-Saxons whose lands they had seized. The main features of its design consisted of a central mound, known as the motte, encircled by a ditch and crowned with a wooden palisade, the whole located within a wide area known as the bailey. This was enclosed in turn by a second earthen mound, which was fortified with further wooden defences and another ditch. Where the lie of the land permitted, both ditches were filled with water. The motte served as the final defensive position in the stronghold, while the bailey provided protection for men, animals and stores. Structures of this kind, fashioned as they were from local materials, and erected by the forced labour of the inhabitants under the ruthless eye of their Norman conquerors, could be put up quite quickly—sometimes in little more than a week.

The new fortress at Windsor formed one of a ring of strongholds built to control the area around London, each separated from its neighbours and from the centre by about 20 miles—the distance of a day's march. The site at Windsor was of exceptional military importance, because it dominated the middle reaches of the Thames,

William I	1066–1087
William II	1087–1100
Henry I	1100–1135
Stephen	1135–1154

LEFT: Reconstruction of a typical Norman fort of the 11th century.

An artificial mound of earth, known as the motte, forms the strongpoint. Encircled by a ditch, and furnished with wooden defences, it is surmounted by a small building also of wood, designed to provide secure living quarters for the garrison commander. Beside the motte stands a wide level area, known as the bailey, bordered with similar defences. Besides giving added protection to the motte this functions as a refuge for men and their animals. Sundry timber-framed buildings within it provide shelter for both. The ditches, here shown dry, are filled with water if the levels permit.

Strongholds of this kind made it possible for relatively small Norman forces to dominate the countryside in the face of a hostile population.

then the main freight route into the interior. The fortifications erected upon it were made unusually long and narrow so as to take advantage of a lengthy escarpment. As a result the outer bailey was only marginally wider than the central motte, which effectively divided it into two separate areas. These were known as the Upper Bailey (to the east, where the ground is higher) and the Lower Bailey (to the west). To give further strength against attack from the west the Lower Bailey was subdivided into two sections by another mound, also surmounted with wooden defences.

Apart from its strategic advantages the site had other attractions: it was on the edge of a vast tract of royal forest, which stretched all the way to the borders of the New Forest created by William the Conqueror in the south-west of Hampshire. The Saxon kings had hunted in these forests, basing themselves upon a small hunting lodge four miles downstream from the new fortress, in an ancient settlement called Windlesora. Their Norman successors, no less keen on the hunt, soon moved house to the greater safety of the fortress, giving it the name of the older settlement.

Of the earliest royal residence within its defences there is now no trace, but we know from contemporary records that King Henry I held court there in 1110, just over 40 years after the conquest. At that time it was only one of many royal residences at which the sovereign might stay during his progresses through the kingdom; but it was sufficiently important to be chosen for the celebration of the king's marriage to his second wife, Adeliza of Brabant and Lower Lorraine, in 1121. This occasion is memorable for a scandalous altercation between the Bishop of Salisbury, in whose diocese Windsor lay, and the Archbishop of Canterbury, both of whom claimed the right to conduct the ceremony. The archbishop carried bigger guns, and won the day. He performed the glittering ceremony on 24 January in the presence of the whole Council of England.

ABOVE: Commissioned soon after the Norman Conquest by Odo Bishop of Bayeux, half-brother of William the Conqueror, the Bayeux Tapestry provides a contemporary record of events leading up to and including the Battle of Hastings.

This episode shows that William wasted no time after landing at Pevensey in constructing a strongpoint of the kind described on the opposite page. At the bidding of one of their new Norman masters, probably Roger de Mortain, another half-brother of the Conqueror, whose right hand seems to indicate that the motte is not high enough, Anglo-Saxon labourers toil to raise it higher. The stylized structure on the summit may represent some kind of fighting platform. The inscription shows that the site of the structure is Hastings, and scenes depicting the battle follow soon after.

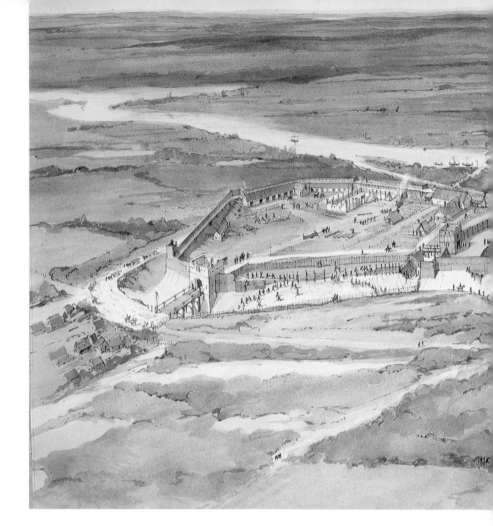

ABOVE RIGHT: Reconstruction of Windsor Castle in its original form about 1080.

Unlike the more typical form shown on page 6 the bailey here is long and narrow, to take advantage of the escarpment on the north side of the hill, and the motte is placed half-way along it instead of to one side, dividing it into two separate areas, the Lower Bailey (on the left) and the Upper Bailey (on the right).

The gateway to the Lower Bailey, the only entrance to the castle and its most vulnerable point, is shown on the extreme left as built in stone (this is conjectural). In the middle of the far side of this bailey a hall is under construction. On the near side of the bailey the white chalk soil is still being excavated from the ditch and piled up to form the defensive earthwork. The outer palisade cannot be erected until the earthwork is finished, and meanwhile a temporary one has been built behind it to protect this area from attack. At the higher (right-hand) end of the bailey a small wooden gateway and palisade defends access to the central area, where the motte stands.

The southern side of the motte is also still under construction, and labourers wind their way up its side carrying loads of chalk soil. The palisade on its summit, and the small building providing quarters for the garrison commander, are complete.

Access from the central area to the Upper (right-hand) Bailey is defended by a further gateway, sited to the left of the stairway leading to the top of the motte. In the middle of the far side of this bailey more spacious living quarters, probably for the king, are under construction.

BELOW RIGHT: The castle during the siege of 1216.

Most of the timber defences have now been replaced by stone walls, erected 50 years earlier by King Henry II. They do not extend to the bottom end of the Lower Bailey (extreme left). All peripheral towers are rectangular, in contrast to those built after the siege, when the stronger semicircular shape was in general use.

The castle was defended for King John against the barons and their French allies by the redoubtable warrior Engelard de Cigogné, so

8

feared by the barons that they had secured a clause in Magna Carta banishing him from the realm. He made 'many fierce sallies, twice cutting the beam of their perrière (stone catapult)'.

Here four 'perrières' are shown in the lines of the besiegers, while the defenders are trying to knock them out with three others, one of which is still being erected.

In front of the Round Tower stands a small new gateway giving direct access to the Upper Bailey. To the right of this a battering ram is in action, protected by a sloping roof. To reduce its efficacy the members of the garrison are lowering a fender.

In the lean-to beside the Great Hall of King Henry II in the Lower Bailey a fire has been started, perhaps ignited by firebrands attached to arrows.

The siege was raised after three months when the king drew off the baronial forces by devastating lands in East Anglia belonging to some of the barons. The damage to the walls was repaired in the following reign.

This fine aerial view of the entire
castle from the south-east invites us
to trace its transformation from a
grim fortress of the 11th century
into the friendly country house
of today.

Not only does the outer shape
remain unchanged from the original
earth and timber stronghold (page 8,
upper illustration) but much of the
perimeter wall erected by King
Henry II (page 8, lower illustration)
with its rectangular towers still
stands, though heavily restored. This
wall presented a forbidding
appearance (see upper illustration
on page 17) until the 17th century,
when the first large windows appear
(page 43), to be followed by the
present more generous array when
King George IV moved the Private
Apartments to this side of the castle
(page 54), and added the formal
garden. In the centre stands the
Round Tower, whose height he
doubled, turning a squat structure
designed for a strictly defensive
function into the dominant feature of
the castle. In front of it stand the
twin towers of Lancaster and York
which he raised astride a new
archway pierced in the castle wall to
admit the carriage-way of the Long
Walk (page 55) into the Upper
Ward. Behind and to the right
extend the State Apartments, where
the personal quarters of the
sovereign lay in earlier times, and
which are now open to the public,
while to the left of the Round Tower
stretches the Lower Ward, with St
George's Chapel, and on its left the
pointed roof of the Curfew Tower,
with the river beyond.

In front of the castle lies the Home
Park, where earlier sovereigns
hunted, while further to the right
stands the chapel of Eton College.
Beyond it the view stretches across
Buckinghamshire to the Chiltern
Hills.

10

Early Plantagenets

Another 50 years were to pass before the royal occupants were able to enjoy the comfort of stone buildings in the castle. To provide this luxury, heavy blocks had to be brought from as far away as Bedfordshire. Some of them were used to construct a private residence on the north side of the Upper Ward: and the principal walls of this structure, overlaid by the decoration of later centuries, actually survive within the framework of the present State Apartments. The remainder was used for a second range of buildings designed for more public purposes in the Lower Ward, including a hall and a chapel.

These buildings were erected by King Henry II, the vigorous founder of the House of Plantagenet. Not long after their completion a rebellion instigated by his sons diverted his energies to military construction, and he set about replacing the timber defences of the castle with stone. For this purpose his masons found a suitable material much nearer to hand—a rugged glacial deposit lying in large boulders in the sandy country 10 miles to the south near Bagshot. So hard that it is impervious to water, this heath stone, as it is called, lasts indefinitely, and is an ideal substance for facing the walls of a fortress. With it he built a wall around the outer perimeter of the castle, following the line of the original earthworks, and furnished with rectangular towers projecting at regular intervals as a defence against scaling. These walls, though heavily restored through the centuries, still stand as the perimeter wall of the castle. The central mound was also surmounted with a collar of stone, to form the so-called Round Tower. Before the outer wall could be completed the king had brought the rebellion under control, and he found it cheaper to pull down the rebel castles rather than spend more money on his own. In consequence the western end of the Lower Ward was left with its timber defences.

Although the walls built by Henry II were never tried in battle during his lifetime they were put to the test on two occasions when the castle was in the possession of his youngest son, John. The first was in 1193, during the reign of Henry's eldest son, King Richard I, when John rebelled against his brother. The castle was duly besieged by the king's forces and some damage was done, but it was still holding out when John reached an arrangement with his brother a month later, and the rebellion came to an end. The second occurred in 1216 when John, now king, having set his seal to Magna Carta in the previous

Henry II 1154–1189
Richard I 1189–1199
John 1199–1216
Henry III 1216–1272

BELOW: Prospect of the castle from the south-south-west, engraved by Wenceslaus Hollar. This 17th-century view points the contrast between the rectangular shape of the eastern towers, on the right, built by King Henry II in the 12th century, and the curved shape of the western, on the left, erected in the 13th century, which formed the last part of the exterior walling to be completed. The tower to the left of the Round Tower owes its curved outline to repairs after the siege of 1216. That to the right of the Round Tower was built a century and a half later, by King Edward III.

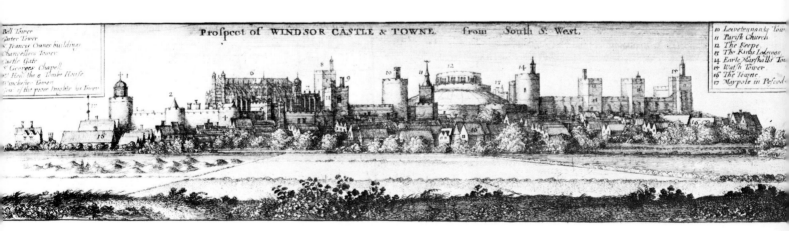

ABOVE: The castle from the north-east, also by Hollar. The appearance of the east wall of the castle at the time this drawing was executed, in the middle of the 17th century, is virtually unchanged from the time of its first construction by King Henry II five centuries earlier. Note the rectangular shape of the towers, and the absence of windows in the main expanse of the wall.

LEFT: The oldest surviving room in the castle, this dungeon is in the basement of the Curfew Tower, which forms part of the last section of the outer defences of the castle to be completed in stone. It was constructed in 1227–30.

13

year, turned the tables on the barons by persuading the Pope to annul the agreement. The barons rebelled, and sought help from the king of France, offering the throne of England to his son. This time the siege lasted for three months, and the defences of the castle took a severe battering. The garrison managed to hold out until the king drew off the besieging troops by sending a large force into East Anglia to devastate the lands of the leading rebel magnates. Later in the same year the king died, to be succeeded by his 10-year-old son, King Henry III. With his death the rebellion was gradually brought under control, and the siege of the castle was not resumed.

Early in the new reign the damage was repaired, and the wall at the western end of the Lower Ward completed. In the half-century since the walls were begun by King Henry II, military architects had learnt that towers with a curved outline were less easy to knock down or undermine than rectangular ones, and afforded a clearer field of fire. The exterior of the towers on the new section was accordingly made semicircular in shape, and so was that of the damaged towers which had to be rebuilt. The basement of one of the new towers, now known as the Curfew Tower, still contains a fine example of a 13th-century dungeon.

With the completion of the defences the king could turn his attention to the domestic accommodation of the castle. The buildings put up by his grandfather in the previous century were cramped and uncomfortable by the standards of the time, and after his marriage to Eleanor of Provence in 1236 he set about providing her with the most up-to-date and luxurious accommodation the age could offer. The work continued for 20 years, until there was, in the words of a chronicler, 'no finer castle in the whole of Europe'. Novelties in the queen's private apartments included windows overlooking the herb garden 'with glass panes which open and shut', and pillars of marble in her chamber. Nurseries were added when her children were born.

Not content with this lavish provision for his family, the king raised a completely new block of royal apartments, for more formal purposes, in the Lower Bailey, next to the great hall built by his grandfather, which he also reconstructed. Beside them he built a chapel, the precursor of the present St George's Chapel. The palace was destroyed by fire at the end of the century, but the chapel survived, and was still standing when King Edward III founded the Order of the Garter in the middle of the following century.

ABOVE: Gilt bronze effigy of King Henry III surmounting his tomb in Westminster Abbey, by William Torel, 1291. The king is shown wearing coronation robes, and his crown was orginally decorated with jewels.

BELOW: Detail from the earliest known representation of the castle. This crude but interesting drawing, made about 1450, shows the Lower Ward before the construction of King Henry VIII's gateway and of the present St George's Chapel. The outline of the earlier chapel erected by King Henry III in 1240–8 is seen in the centre, and the 12th-century predecessor of King Henry's gateway appears at top right. (From a manuscript in the Fellows' Library at Eton College.)

ABOVE: This arcade of 13th-century arches, filled in during the following century to form the south wall of the Dean's Cloister, originally stood in King Henry III's chapel.

LEFT: Originally forming the western entrance to King Henry III's chapel, this door, decorated with iron scrollwork fashioned by Gilebertus in about 1246, is now at the extreme east end of St George's Chapel.

Later Plantagenets

King Edward III, who was born at Windsor, decided to found a new order of chivalry to celebrate his martial victories, in the course of which the kings of both Scotland and France had been brought as prisoners to Windsor. His original intention was to revive King Arthur's Knights of the Round Table, and work started on a circular building in the Upper Ward of the castle, doubtless intended to accommodate the table. Before the work was finished, however, the king changed his mind, and decided instead to found the Order of the Garter.

Many explanations have been offered for the choice of so intimate a garment as the emblem of the country's leading order of chivalry. The traditional story is that at a ball to celebrate the capture of Calais in 1347 a garter worn by Joan, Countess of Salisbury, a celebrated beauty who may have been the king's mistress and certainly married his eldest son, the Black Prince, fell to the ground. When the king picked it up, some of those around him smiled at what they took to be an amorous gesture. This led the king to utter the celebrated words *'Honi soit qui mal y pense'* ('Shame on him who thinks evil of it'), adding that they would soon see that garter advanced to so high an honour that they would be happy to wear it themselves.

Having determined, for whatever reason, to found this order, the king decided to provide a worthy setting for it by reconstructing the royal apartments in the Upper Ward. Henry III's sumptuous domestic apartments were accordingly demolished, to make way for something even more spectacular, spacious enough to do duty as well for the more formal apartments in the Lower Ward which had been destroyed by fire. The principal place of assembly in this new building was St George's Hall, where the Knights Companion of the new order met on St George's Day for their ceremonial banquet. A new gatehouse at the entrance to the Upper Ward, which was raised to guard access to these apartments, survives to this day under the misleading name of the Norman Gateway.

As a place of worship for his new order the king made use of the chapel built by Henry III in the Lower Ward, reconstructing its furnishings and extending its dedication to include St George, who was to be the patron saint of the new order. Around it, on the site of King Henry's former apartments, he built extensive quarters for the clergy, many of which still stand.

So thorough were the works carried out for this king that the basic accommodation remained unchanged for 300 years, as long a span as has elapsed between King Charles II and the present day. Immense quantities of stone were brought from widely separated counties, some from as far afield as Yorkshire, and no less than four woods were demolished to provide timber. 'Almost all the masons and carpenters throughout the whole of England', wrote a chronicler, 'were brought to that building, so that hardly anyone could have a good mason or carpenter except in secret, on account of the king's prohibition.' In 1360 alone the sheriffs of 13 counties were ordered to send 568 masons. The only monarch in the history of the castle to match this extravagance was King George IV, four and a half centuries later.

Edward I 1272–1307
Edward II 1307–1327
Edward III 1327–1377
Richard II ....1377–1399.

FACING PAGE ABOVE: Detail from a bird's-eye view of the castle engraved by Wenceslaus Hollar in the mid-17th century, showing the Apartments of State erected by King Edward III 300 years earlier. The original St George's Hall, numbered 17 on the roof, is on the right of the main block, facing the quadrangle.

FACING PAGE BELOW: The interior of the original St George's Hall, built by King Edward III in 1362–5. This engraving, also by Hollar, shows the banquet of the Knights of the Garter. King Charles II is seated alone on a dais at the far end, and the Knights Companion are at the long table on the left.

A few years after these engravings were made King Charles ordered the demolition of most of King Edward's apartments, to make way for a new residence in the Baroque style.

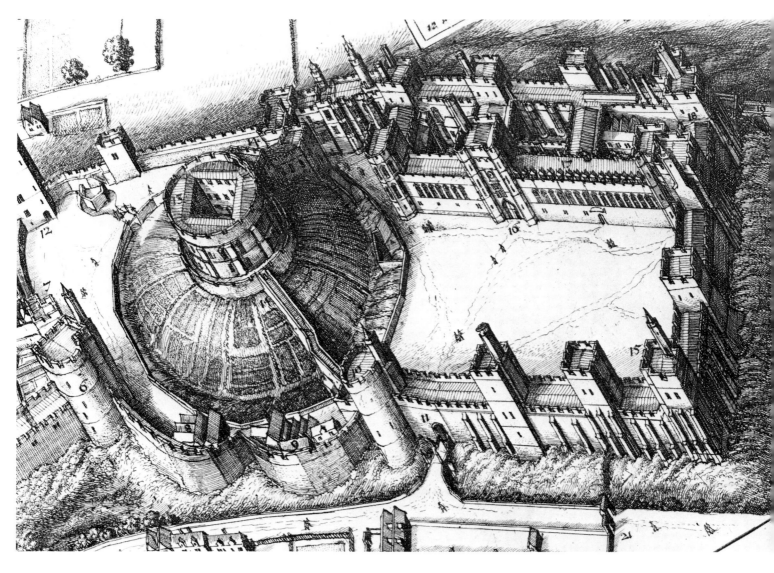

18

FACING PAGE ABOVE: St George's Chapel, founded in 1475 by King Edward IV and completed 50 years later by King Henry VIII, is one of the finest examples of the Perpendicular style of late Gothic architecture.

FACING PAGE BELOW: The Albert Memorial Chapel stands on the site of the earlier chapel built by King Henry III (see page 14). Built by King Henry VII in the late 15th century as a Lady Chapel for St George's Chapel, and subsequently intended for use as a tomb-house, it was converted by Queen Victoria into a memorial for her husband the Prince Consort. See page 81.

RIGHT: The so-called Norman Gateway, built by King Edward III in 1359–60 to replace an earlier gateway defending access to the Upper Ward.

BELOW: The upper end of Castle Hill, showing the curved outline of King Edward III Tower (1367–8).

BELOW RIGHT: Portrait of King Edward III, holding the two-handed sword which hung above his stall in King Henry III's chapel and which is preserved in St George's Chapel. The painting was made in 1615.

Lancaster and York

King Edward's immediate successors were content with the castle as they found it. His grandson King Richard II told his clerk of the works, who happened, surprisingly, to be the poet Chaucer, to repair the chapel, but little or nothing seems to have been done. King Edward's splendid quadrangle was the setting for the great court of chivalry summoned by King Richard in 1398 which led to the banishment of Henry, Duke of Hereford, soon to return and seize the throne as King Henry IV—an act of usurpation which eventually led to the Wars of the Roses. Perhaps for this reason the new king showed little affection for the place. His son King Henry V was preoccupied for most of his reign with wars in France, and the pious King Henry VI preferred to spend his money on his religious and scholarly foundations of Eton College across the river and King's College at Cambridge. So it is not surprising to learn that at this time 'for default of coverture it raineth within diverse and many places of our castle at Windsor where, through the same, places be fallen in great and ruinous decay'.

It was left to that unfortunate monarch's successor, King Edward IV, at whose bidding he probably met his death, to replace King Henry III's now dilapidated chapel with a house for the Deity which for the first time bore comparison with the magnificence of the sovereign's apartments. King Edward also intended the new structure to outdo the fine chapel which his fallen rival had erected across the river at Eton, and even took preliminary steps to dissolve the foundation of Eton College itself and merge it with that of St George at Windsor, a course in which he did not, fortunately, persist. The building, which he started in 1475, but which was not completed for 50 years, is one of the finest examples of that peculiarly English style called Perpendicular, and the principal glory of the castle.

House of Lancaster

Henry IV 1399–1413

Henry V 1413–1422

Henry VI 1422–1461

House of York

Edward IV 1461–1483

Edward V 1483

Richard III 1483–1485

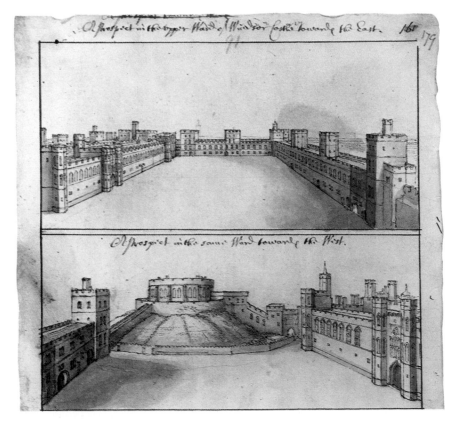

FACING PAGE: Anonymous portraits of four 15th-century kings of England which have probably been in the Royal Collection since the reign of King Henry VIII. All show a strong Flemish influence and may have come from the same workshop. That of King Edward IV seems to have been painted from life; the sources of the other likenesses have not been established. The portraits above are of King Henry VI (left) and King Henry V. Those below are of King Edward IV (left) and King Richard III.

LEFT: The quadrangle in the Upper Ward showing the buildings erected by King Edward III in the 14th century, shortly before their reconstruction by King Charles II. King Edward's State Apartments are on the left of the upper illustration. The lower illustration shows the Round Tower, with the south-west corner of the State Apartments on the right. The drawings are by Wenceslaus Hollar.

HENRY THE SIXTH

HENRY THE FIFTH

K Edward

FACING PAGE: Modern photograph of the choir of St George's Chapel looking east. The first part of the chapel to be constructed, it was all but finished, with a wooden roof, at the death of its founder, King Edward IV, in 1483. The fine vault was added just over 20 years later by King Henry VII.

The banner of each Knight of the Garter, bearing his coat of arms, hangs above his stall. Beneath each banner, and over the canopy above the stall, stands his crest. Below the canopy some of the gilt stall plates (see below) can just be discerned.

The vault beneath the inscribed stone in the centre foreground contains the remains of King Henry VIII, his third wife Queen Jane Seymour, King Charles I and an infant child of Queen Anne.

To the left of the east window (1863) stands the wooden oriel built by Henry VIII to enable his first queen, Catherine of Aragon, to attend mass in privacy. It was put to a similar purpose by Queen Victoria after the death of her husband in 1861.

ABOVE: The interior of St George's Chapel in 1819, looking westwards from the altar. Watercolour by C. Wild.

During repairs to the chapel in 1921–30 the elegant organ case shown here, which was designed by Henry Emlyn and presented by King George III, was replaced by a new arrangement divided into two parts and placed on either side of the screen, so that the full length of the vaulted roof can now be seen from either end of the chapel without obstruction.

RIGHT: When a new Knight of the Garter is created a gilt metal plate is engraved and enamelled or painted in colour with his armorial bearings and affixed to the back of his stall. The magnificent array of these stall plates, which date from the 14th century to the present day, forms an assemblage of original heraldic work without parallel in this medium. The earliest plates are those cut to the shape of the design.

ABOVE: This watercolour by Joseph Nash shows the scene outside St George's Chapel on a Sunday morning in 1840. The choir emerges from the Horseshoe Cloister on its way to morning service, the congregation assembles outside the south porch, and a military band plays on the grass. Military Knights in their scarlet uniforms and cocked hats mingle with others moving towards the chapel.

LEFT: Erected in 1359/60 by King Edward III as a belfry for the predecessor of the present St George's Chapel, the tower in the centre of this 18th-century watercolour by Paul Sandby has been the residence of the Governor of the Military Knights (see page 27) since the days of Mary Tudor. To the left of the tower stand lodgings built for the clergy at the same time, and allotted by Queen Mary to the Knights.

The Tudors

When King Henry VII assumed the crown on the field of Bosworth he inherited a castle whose domestic apartments were already somewhat antiquated—having been standing for well over a century—and whose principal chapel was under construction. He continued the building of the chapel, and brought the domestic apartments up to date by using the only remaining vacant plot in the Upper Ward for a new building to house his queen, Elizabeth of York, and her nursery. The king's marriage to the Yorkist heiress had at last united the opposing factions of the Wars of the Roses, that grim conflict stemming from the fateful court of chivalry summoned by King Richard II in the quadrangle nearly a century earlier, in which most of the country's aristocracy had perished. The well-being of the new king's family was accordingly of cardinal dynastic importance, and he took steps to provide them with modern and well-appointed accommodation. Although the queen was fated to suffer a premature death giving birth to their seventh child, the dynasty which they founded lasted for over a century, and the Stuart dynasty which succeeded it was descended from their eldest daughter, Margaret.

Three years after the queen's death King Henry entertained the young King Philip I of Castile and his queen, Joanna, at Windsor on their way from the Netherlands to take possession of their kingdom. The visiting sovereign was given lodgings in the new building, and from its windows found himself regaled on several occasions with the gruesome spectacle of horse-baiting, enacted for his diversion in the courtyard below. Also visible from its windows was a tennis court, in which he was invited to play, while the middle-aged English king looked on.

The chapel was finished by Henry's surviving son, King Henry VIII, who also contributed the present handsome gateway to the castle. The large room above this gateway served for nearly three centuries as a gaol for prisoners convicted of offences within the castle and the forest.

The security and prestige which a fortress confers on its inmates are gained at the cost of certain amenities. Designed to keep strangers out, its walls also cut off the inhabitants from the surrounding countryside. There is no garden in which to stroll on the spur of the moment, and any excursion into the grounds becomes an expedition. The sole link with the outside world is the heavily defended main gateway, sometimes, as at Windsor, supplemented by a smaller postern gate. Further breaches in the walls can only be made as the defensive needs of the castle grow less stringent.

By the end of the middle ages the military usefulness of castles was in fact declining as the destructive power of the cannon increased, and in 1533 Henry VIII saw no reason against making a direct way from his private apartments on the north side of the castle to the Little Park by which it was surrounded. This involved a structural change which would never have been contemplated in the heyday of siege warfare. The wall on this side was virtually impregnable because it sprang directly from the top of the cliff on which it stood. The king now had a wooden platform or 'wharf' built along the clifftop at the foot of the wall, linked to his private apartments by an outside staircase and

BELOW: The building erected by King Henry VII as an addition to the private apartments of his queen, Elizabeth of York, c. 1497. The saloon on the first floor now forms part of the Royal Library. From a drawing by F. Mackenzie.

leading to a bridge over the ditch at the eastern end. He could now make his way directly from his apartments to the Little Park, where 'His Grace, every afternoon, when the weather is anything fair, doth ride forth on hawking, or walketh, and cometh not in again till it be late in the evening'.

The reign of King Henry VIII stands exactly half-way between the foundation of the castle at the end of the 11th century and the present day: and it is at this time that we see the beginnings of the Royal Collection as it is now known. Perhaps the most interesting series of works of art of this period which it contains, and which may well have belonged to King Henry, is the famous group of drawings by Holbein depicting persons about the court. Holbein was court painter to the king, and had the use of a studio in Whitehall Palace. When he died suddenly of the plague in 1543 these drawings were left in his studio, and presumably came directly into the king's possession; at all events they are recorded as having belonged to his son, King Edward VI, who came to the throne four years later and only survived for a further six. These dazzling portraits, 80 in number, after two brief periods in private hands, returned to the Royal Collection in the late 17th century and are now in the Royal Library at Windsor. A selection of them is always on show in the public exhibition beside the entrance to the State Apartments.

A masterpiece of a different kind dating from this reign is the magnificent suit of armour made for the king at Greenwich in about 1540, and exhibited on the Grand Staircase.

Next to the king's new gateway stands a range of lodgings built under the terms of his will in the reign of his eldest daughter, Queen Mary I, for a body of men then known as the Poor Knights. This foundation was originally instituted by King Edward III in association with the Order of the Garter to provide board and lodging for soldiers who had served in the wars with distinction. Their only duty was to represent the Knights of the Garter at daily services in the chapel. Renamed Military Knights in 1833 by King William IV, their successors still occupy these lodgings, and attend services in St George's Chapel on Sundays and on great ceremonial occasions, wearing their unique scarlet uniform.

A century after King Henry VII had added his new wing to the royal apartments in the Upper Ward, his other grand-daughter, Queen Elizabeth I, made a further addition. In the small vacant space between his building and the 14th-century gatehouse which guards the entrance to the Upper Ward she built one of the fashionable long galleries, in which to display her pictures and fine furniture and take exercise in wet weather. She came to Windsor regularly in late summer to escape the plague in London: but liked it so much that even when a page died of 'the sickness' in the castle she stayed for several more weeks, occupying her extraordinary intellectual powers in translating Boethius's *de Consolatione*. Not that this talented and energetic queen spent all her time indoors. That she participated actively in field sports is shown by a letter from her secretary Lord Burghley recording the gift to the Archbishop of Canterbury of a stag she had herself killed at Windsor. To improve access from her private apartments to the Little Park, where she often hunted, she replaced her father's wooden 'wharf' with a fine terrace of stone.

Meanwhile the main royal apartments of King Edward III, now more than two centuries old, were basically unchanged. Life in these vast and rugged chambers must have been far from comfortable by the

ABOVE: Suit of armour made for King Henry VIII in the Royal Armouries at Greenwich, *c.* 1540, and displayed on the Grand Staircase (page 74).

FACING PAGE TOP: Miniatures of Henry VII and Henry VIII by Nicholas Hilliard. The former is derived from the image of the king painted by Holbein on the wall of the Privy Chamber, for which the cartoon is at the National Portrait Gallery.

FACING PAGE CENTRE: The 'wharf' or wooden terrace built on the north side of the royal apartments by King Henry VIII. Detail from a drawing by Hoefnagel, *c.* 1570.

FACING PAGE BOTTOM: The gateway erected by King Henry VIII in 1509. The houses flanking the castle wall were demolished in the 19th century. From an 18th-century watercolour by Paul Sandby.

Three studies by Hans Holbein the Younger, made for a group of the More family painted in 1526–8.

LEFT: Sir Thomas More, Lord Chancellor to King Henry VIII, and Holbein's first patron in England. More was executed in 1535 on a charge of treason based on perjured evidence. This drawing, one of Holbein's ablest character studies, is connected with the oil painting of More in the Frick Collection, New York.

BELOW LEFT: His son John More; an outstanding study exemplifying the artist's brilliant use of black chalk.

BELOW RIGHT: Anne Cresacre, John More's wife.

standards of today. The ceilings were usually coated with yellow ochre and (reversing the colour schemes of today) the bare stone walls covered with whitewash. Some warmth and colour would be lent to the principal rooms by cloth of Arras (tapestry). The floor covering in most rooms was rushes, to which new layers were added from time to time, while food and other detritus rotted underneath. It is not surprising that the court, living on this vast deep-litter system, found it necessary to move on to other houses at regular intervals, or that the medieval houses of the great were always built around courtyards, where herbs were grown to sweeten the air.

In the smaller private rooms of the monarch the effect of these offensive conditions was overlaid by greater luxury, such as silk and linen hangings, carpets and, rarest of all, a bath. Visitors of state would also be offered comforts of this order. When King Edward IV received the Governor of the Netherlands at Windsor in 1472, he conducted him to 'three chambers of pleasance, all hung with white silk and linen cloth, and the floors covered with carpets. There was . . . a bed . . . of as good down as could be got, and sheets of Raines (fine linen from Rennes in Brittany) also fine fustians: the counterpoint cloth of gold, furred with ermine . . . The 2nd chamber was all white [with] a couch with feather beds . . . hanged with a tent (canopy) . . . and . . . a cupboard. In the 3rd chamber was . . . a bath or two, covered with tents of white cloth.' The chronicler goes on to relate that when the king and queen had retired, the Governor and the Lord Chamberlain went, in the presence of their combined retinue, to the bath. 'And when they had been in their baths as long as was their pleasure they had ginger, divers syrups, comfits and Hippocras (spiced wine), and then they went to bed.'

Such luxury required elaborate preparation: and when the boy-king Edward VI was virtually kidnapped by the Duke of Somerset in 1549 and spirited away at night from Hampton Court to Windsor under heavy guard, no preparations had been made. Having caught cold on the nocturnal ride, he found nothing to relieve the dank gloom of the medieval chambers, and would have moved on if he could. 'Methinks I am in prison', he confided to a member of his retinue, 'here be no galleries nor no gardens to walk in.' The younger of his two sisters, Elizabeth, was, as we have seen, to rectify the first deficiency, but the main rooms continued to stand for another 80 years, and were described by Evelyn during the Commonwealth as 'melancholy and of ancient appearance'. And if conditions for monarchs were uncomfortable those for courtiers could be primitive. 'The Maids of Honour', we are told in the reign of Queen Elizabeth I, 'desire to have their chamber ceiled (i.e. provided with a ceiling) and the partition that is of boards there to be made higher, for that their servants look over.' The Squires of the Body were in no better case: their chamber was 'ruinous and cold', and besides lacking a proper ceiling needed to be 'boarded underfoot'.

BELOW: Queen Mary I, from a coloured engraving in the Royal Library after an oil painting by Hans Eworth in the Society of Antiquaries. Queen Mary was the elder daughter of King Henry VIII and the only child of his marriage to Queen Catherine of Aragon.

ABOVE: King Edward VI shortly before his accession to the throne in January 1547. The jewel suspended from the chain around his shoulders is decorated with the crown and feathers of the Prince of Wales. The artist of this portrait, doubtless painted for King Henry VIII and attributed to Holbein for many years, is unknown. The technique appears to be Flemish, or Franco-Flemish.

King Edward was the only son of King Henry VIII. His mother, Jane Seymour, died in giving him birth. He came to the throne at the age of nine, and died shortly before his sixteenth birthday.

RIGHT: Portrait of Queen Elizabeth I by Nicholas Hilliard. The exquisite miniatures of this remarkable artist, son of a goldsmith, were intended to be regarded as jewels rather than paintings.

FACING PAGE: Queen Elizabeth I when princess. This charming portrait, almost certainly by the same hand as the portrait of King Edward VI, was probably painted for King Henry VIII about 1546. The small book in the princess's hands, and the larger one at her side, are tokens of her intellectual abilities.

TOP: Detail from a 17th-century engraving by Wenceslaus Hollar after a drawing by Christopher Wren of the north front of the castle, showing the fine stone terrace built for Queen Elizabeth I to replace Henry VIII's wooden 'wharf'.

ABOVE: Queen Elizabeth's Gallery and the 14th-century inner gateway (miscalled the Norman Gateway) by John Buckler. The gallery, which links the Norman Gateway to Henry VII's Tower (page 25), now forms part of the Royal Library.

The Stuarts

Notwithstanding these discomforts successive monarchs liked the castle for its excellent hunting, both in the Little Park surrounding the castle and in the Great Park further afield. When King James VI of Scotland, on coming south to claim his English inheritance as King James I, had made a reconnaissance of all his houses, he wasted no time in returning to Windsor with his queen and elder son, undeterred by an unedifying squabble about accommodation between the English and Scottish lords which had marred his first hours in the castle. His visit was the start of a regular series which lasted until the end of his reign.

His son King Charles I, who first set eyes on Windsor when he travelled south from Scotland at the age of three, was no less devoted a visitor: but he had other interests besides the hunt. Attracted to the arts at an early age, he was dazzled by the wealth of the collections in Spain, where he had journeyed at the impressionable age of 22 on an unsuccessful suit for the hand of the Spanish king's daughter. Already the owner of a notable collection, he now improved it to such effect that Rubens called him 'the greatest amateur of paintings among the princes of the world', and spoke of 'the incredible quantity of excellent pictures, statues, and ancient inscriptions which are to be found at this court'. Prominent among these was Rubens's own magnificent self-portrait which he painted at the king's request, and which now hangs at Windsor. Another living artist patronized by the king was Rubens's pupil Van Dyck, who painted the celebrated triple portrait of the king— commissioned so that the fashionable sculptor Bernini could carve his bust in Rome—and the no less famous group of his five eldest children, both also at Windsor. The variety and richness of this collection, which contained works by many other artists and which the king kept chiefly at Whitehall Palace in London, has never been equalled by any other single collector. His tastes were also reflected in the constructional works which he ordered to be carried out at Windsor, which included a new group of statuary for the fountain in the middle of the great quadrangle 'whereon shall be placed the statues

BELOW: Bird's-eye view of the castle from the north, made for King James I by John Norden in 1607. In the left foreground stand the 14th-century royal apartments of King Edward III, with King Henry VII's Tower and Queen Elizabeth's Gallery on their right. Between them and the Round Tower is a tennis court. The fountain in the middle of the quadrangle provided the water supply. In the right foreground stands St George's Chapel.

Old Master Drawings in the Royal Collection which may have belonged to King Charles I.

ABOVE: Michelangelo: The Virgin and Child with St John. Study in black chalk.

ABOVE RIGHT: Domenico Ghirlandaio: Head of an Old Woman, drawn in metal point heightened with white, before 1500.

RIGHT: Raphael: The Three Graces. Study in red chalk, about 1516, for a group in a fresco of the Marriage of Cupid and Psyche in the Farnesina, Rome.

FACING PAGE: Michelangelo: The Risen Christ. Study in black chalk, c. 1532.

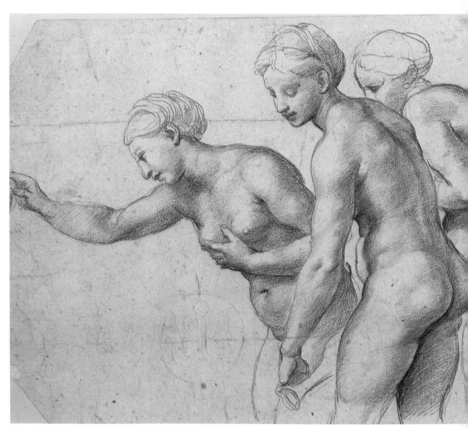

of Hercules worrying of Antaeus as if by squeezing of him, ye water comes out of his mouth'. This was never completed, because of the Civil War.

When conflict broke out in 1642 the king retired to York, and Windsor was swiftly occupied by Parliamentary forces with orders 'to take some especial care of Windsor Castle'. They did. Their first act was to break into the treasury of St George's Chapel and remove all the 'rich chased and other plate made sacred for the service of God'. The clergy were evicted from their houses, and the chapel plundered. One of the objects taken was the coat of mail of King Edward IV, together with his surcoat of crimson velvet embroidered with gold and pearls and decorated with rubies, which had hung over his burial place since his funeral, and which has never been seen since. The Lady Chapel, built on the site of Henry III's old chapel, was converted into a magazine. This done, they turned the castle into a military headquarters and a prison for captured royalists. Life for those who remained was not made easier by a mutiny of Parliamentary troops whose pay was in arrears.

A spirited attempt by the king's nephew, the dashing royalist commander Prince Rupert of the Rhine, to capture the castle in 1642 was easily foiled. His cavalry had no difficulty in overrunning the town, but were stopped short by the walls of the castle. Against these he ranged four guns from the Eton side of the river, while his men tried to dig in at the foot of the walls. But their trenches were soon knocked to bits and they withdrew, saying that they would willingly fight for Prince Rupert against men, but not against stone walls. This was the last occasion on which the walls of Windsor Castle performed the military function for which they were designed.

The king did not see his castle again until he was brought back to it in captivity. On being removed to Hampton Court he managed to escape. Soon afterwards a meeting at Windsor of the leaders of the Parliamentary army, including Cromwell, took the fateful decision 'that the king should be prosecuted for his life as a criminal person'. He was recaptured, eventually escorted back to Windsor, where he spent his last Christmas, and taken to London in January 1649 for trial and execution. After being exposed to public view for many days in a room in Whitehall his body was carried back to Windsor. It lay for the first night in his bedchamber, and for the next in the (unoccupied) Deanery, from where it was taken to St George's Chapel for burial. The interment was conducted in silence as the Parliamentary authorities forbade the use of the Book of Common Prayer.

The king's death was the signal for the dispersal of his possessions, and his great collection of pictures was sold to provide funds for the Parliamentary forces. Some were returned to the Royal Collection after the restoration of his son King Charles II, but many were sent abroad, and are now in collections overseas. The king's residences, including Windsor Castle, were not themselves sold, but retained for the use of the Lord Protector, Oliver Cromwell.

The captivity and execution of the king led to a breakdown of law and order in Windsor Forest. First the local inhabitants, and then the Parliamentary soldiers, killed the deer and tore down the fences. In the castle itself there was an influx of squatters, whose ejection at the restoration of the monarchy in 1660 caused considerable hardship.

With the return from exile of King Charles II the threads of life in the castle were resumed. The Deanery and the Cloisters were re-occupied by the clergy, the king came down to hunt and the Knights

ABOVE: Contemporary cameo portrait of a Roman of classical times, possibly the Emperor Claudius (1st century A.D.). This remarkable portrait, which has survived almost intact from the days of the Roman Empire, belonged to King Charles I.

FACING PAGE ABOVE: Triple portrait of King Charles I, commissioned from Sir Anthony Van Dyck in 1635 to enable the sculptor Gian Lorenzo Bernini to make a bust of the king in Rome. It was brought back from Italy in 1802 and purchased by King George IV 20 years later. The bust was destroyed in the fire of Whitehall Palace in 1698, but a copy survives at Windsor.

FACING PAGE BELOW LEFT: Rubens: Self-portrait, painted for King Charles I in 1623.

FACING PAGE BELOW RIGHT: Portrait of Queen Henrietta Maria, consort of King Charles I, by Van Dyck. Painted for the king, probably in 1632.

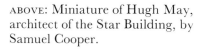
ABOVE: Miniature of Hugh May, architect of the Star Building, by Samuel Cooper.

ABOVE RIGHT: The Star Building, erected by King Charles II in 1675–80 to replace the 14th-century apartments of King Edward III and so called because of the large star of the Order of the Garter in the centre of its façade, is on the left of this detail from an engraving by Johannes Kip after a drawing by Leonard Knyff.

FACING PAGE ABOVE: The interior of St George's Hall after its reconstruction for King Charles II by Hugh May. From a watercolour by Charles Wild (1819). The frescoes, by the Neapolitan artist Antonio Verrio, depict (on the wall) King Edward III receiving his royal prisoners King David of Scotland and King John of France, while the Black Prince rides in a triumphal car, and (on the ceiling) King Charles in allegorical splendour.

FACING PAGE BELOW: The chapel designed for King Charles II by Hugh May, from a watercolour by Charles Wild (1819). The frescoes are by Verrio, and the wood-carvings by Grinling Gibbons and his associates. This room and St Georges Hall were demolished in King George IV's reconstruction.

RIGHT: Equestrian statue of King Charles II, cast by Josias Ibach and erected in the Quadrangle of the castle in 1680. The carved stone panels on the base are by Grinling Gibbons.

Only three rooms in this elegant palace have survived. The most striking is the King's Dining Room, set midway between the apartments of the king and those of his Portuguese queen, Catherine of Braganza. Here the subject fittingly chosen for Verrio's ceiling was a banquet of the gods, while Gibbons's exquisite carvings portray the raw material of the feast in the shape of fruit, game, fish and shellfish. The other two rooms to survive are on Queen Catherine's side of the building—her Presence and Audience Chambers. None of the larger rooms which Hugh May remodelled in the medieval building has been spared, but we know what many of them looked like from watercolours made when they were still almost unchanged early in the 19th century. The diarist John Evelyn was astounded by them. Of one he writes: 'The Chapel of the Resurrection, where the figure of the Ascension is in my opinion comparable to the paintings of any of the most famous Roman masters: the Last Supper also over the Altar . . . nor less the stupendous, and beyond all description, the incomparable carving of our Gibbons who is (without controversy) the greatest master, both for invention and rareness of work, that the world had in any age. Verrio the painter's invention is likewise admirable . . . and if the walls hold (which is the only doubt, by reason of the salts, which in time, and in this moist climate prejudices the work) will preserve his name to ages.' The walls held, but sadly the ceiling did not, and this and all the other larger rooms were completely remodelled in a later reconstruction.

To provide a fortress standing on the edge of a cliff with a garden worthy of a country house is well-nigh impossible and King Charles did not attempt it. The best he could do was to arrange direct access from his north-facing apartments to the gentle slopes on the east and south by constructing a wide terrace at the foot of his new building (replacing the narrower one built by Queen Elizabeth a century earlier, which had to be demolished to make way for the new building) and extending it round the rest of the Upper Ward. The slopes to which the new terrace led were too exposed for a garden: but the eastern ones were flat enough for a bowling green—and bowls was a sport at which the king excelled; while on the south side, where the terrace ended, he arranged the ultimate requirement of the country house—the vista. This took the form of an avenue linking the castle to a low range of hills lying three miles to the south in the Great Park. Invisible from the windows of his own rooms on the north side of the quadrangle, this impressive addition to the scenery still gave pleasure to other royal eyes, as he granted the rooms on the south and east side, previously used by household and for offices, to his brother the Duke of York (later King James II). The promotion of these rooms to royal occupation is marked by the appearance in the walls, hitherto forbiddingly bare, of spacious windows similar to those designed for the king's side of the building. The castle no longer frowned, but smiled. The threat of the fortress had been transformed into the welcome of the country house.

Now that the building had lost much of its military aspect it offered a more congenial setting for works of art: and King Charles II was the first monarch to bring some of his important pieces to Windsor, instead of keeping most of them in London. Among the more striking of his possessions now in the castle is the splendid set of silver furniture presented to him by the City of London in about 1670. It was probably also during this reign that the celebrated volume of drawings by Leonardo da Vinci, which had been brought to England during

ABOVE: The Queen's Presence Chamber, another of the three rooms in Charles II's palace which largely retains its original appearance. The painting on the ceiling, again by Verrio, portrays his queen, Catherine of Braganza, in allegorical scenes.

RIGHT: The south front of the Upper Ward. The towers and walls on the south-east corner are pierced by the spacious windows added when this part of the castle received its first royal occupant, James, Duke of York, brother of King Charles II and later King James II.

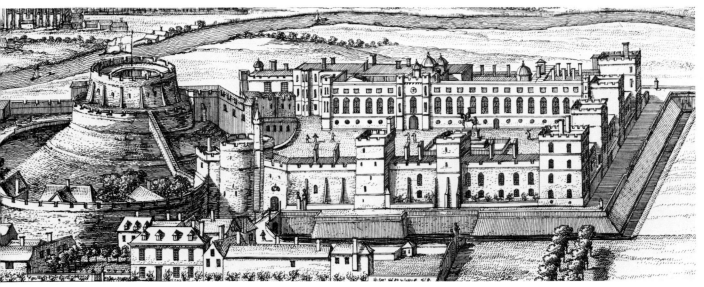

The drawings on these two pages are by Leonardo da Vinci and were probably acquired by King Charles II.

LEFT: Five grotesque heads. This striking drawing has been well known for four centuries through copies and engravings.

BELOW LEFT: Dissections of the skull. The record made by Leonardo of his anatomical dissections is not only remarkable for its brilliant draughtsmanship, but also far ahead of his time in the clear and accurate presentation of anatomical detail.

BELOW RIGHT: Study of plants. Often used in the foreground of his paintings, Leonardo's representations of plants show his usual precision of observation. The principal plant depicted here is the Star of Bethlehem.

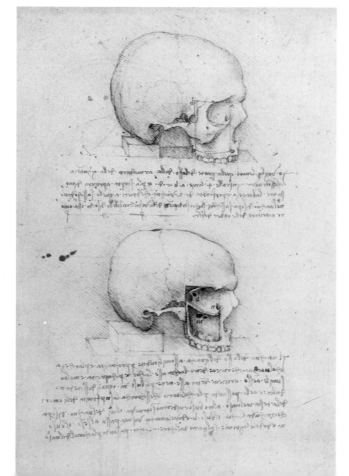

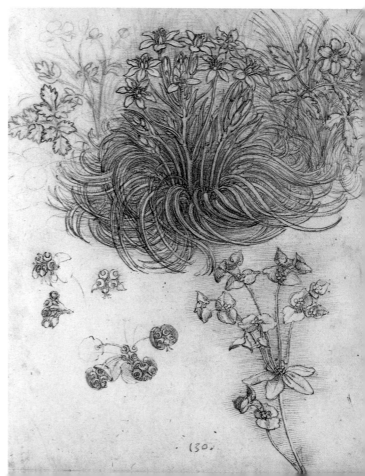

Charles I's reign by the famous collector Thomas Howard, Earl of Arundel, joined the Royal Collection. These drawings, about 600 in number, are among the greatest treasures of the castle. A selection of them is always on view in the Exhibition of Drawings.

Nothing was done to the fabric of the castle in the short reigns of the remaining Stuart sovereigns, but we know that at least one had contemplated changes of the most radical kind. If King William III had not died at the early age of 51 the building might have completely lost its character as a fortress, since he had invited Sir Christopher Wren to remodel the south front after the manner of his additions to Hampton Court. Wren's designs, preserved in the library of All Souls College, would have put the final touches to King Charles II's dream of transforming the castle into a country house, but would have made an absurdity of such vestiges of the medieval structure as were to remain on that side of the building.

King William's sister-in-law Queen Anne had a great affection for Windsor. Before she came to the throne she and her Danish husband stayed in houses near the south front of the castle, at first in Burford House, built by her uncle King Charles II for Nell Gwynn and inherited by their son the Duke of St Albans, and subsequently at a 'neat little seat' which she purchased close to the castle wall. It was here in 1700 that her only surviving son, William, Duke of Gloucester, died shortly after his 11th birthday, a calamity which spelt the end of the Stuart dynasty and led to the Act of Settlement, under which the Elector of Hanover succeeded to the throne as King George I in 1714.

After her accession Queen Anne retained her affection for this house, to which 'she would daily withdraw from the royal lodgings and the state and splendour of a victorious court to enjoy a happy retirement'. One of its attractions for her was that, unlike the castle, it had a garden: but this deficiency in the older building she now took steps to rectify. In 1711 she instructed the landscape gardener Henry Wise to design an elegant formal garden, complete with large ornamental pool, on the low ground lying to the north between the foot of the hill on which the castle stands and the river. This garden was abandoned by her Hanoverian successors, and its life was cruelly short. The pool was eventually filled in, and to the superficial glance its site, which now serves as a sports ground for the town, betrays no sign of its existence. But its ghost survives in the aerial photographs of today, which show paths, pools and avenues corresponding exactly to Wise's plans.

The queen's other contribution to Windsor was more permanent: she started the racecourse at Ascot, where the Royal Meeting in June continues to this day in the presence of the sovereign, who drives to the course in a procession of open carriages.

It was in a small boudoir on the first floor of King Henry VII's building, overlooking the area destined for her garden, that Queen Anne received a messenger from the Duke of Marlborough bearing tidings of the victory of Blenheim in 1704. In recognition of his services the queen subsequently granted the duke a perpetual lease of her ancient estate of Woodstock, north of Oxford, which had been a royal possession since soon after the Norman Conquest, and on which he built Blenheim Palace. As token rent for this lease the duke delivered to the sovereign each year a standard bearing the arms of the king of France, over whom his armies had triumphed. This rent is still paid today, and the current standard hangs over the duke's bust in the Queen's Guard Chamber.

ABOVE: Study for the head of Leda in Leonardo's painting (now lost) of Leda and the Swan. Note the intricate delineation of the hair.

45

ABOVE: The Queen's Audience
Chamber.

The last of the three rooms in
King Charles II's Baroque palace
which retains its 17th-century

appearance, this is where his queen,
Catherine of Braganza, gave
audience. Here visitors were ushered
in from the Presence Chamber next
door. On the ceiling she is again

depicted in allegory by Verrio.

No doubt she had a throne in this room. Queen Anne, who unlike Catherine was a Queen Regnant, certainly did. It is described as 'a magnificent throne with a canopy of fine English velvet, on which are two plumes of fine feathers'.

King Charles hung tapestries in both chambers, but the present magnificent series is of later date. Woven in the Gobelins factory in France between 1779 and 1785, they are based on paintings by J. F. de Troy of the story of Esther.

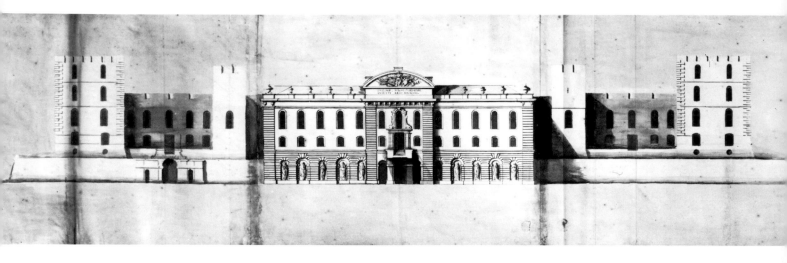

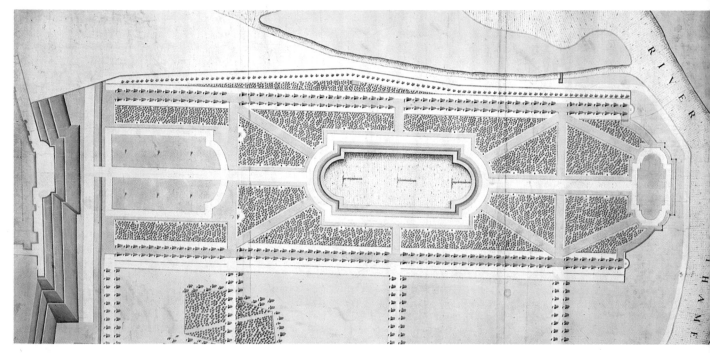

48

RIGHT: Queen Anne, by Sir Godfrey Kneller. This portrait is the model from which the queen's head was taken for the coinage and for medals.

BELOW: Ascot Races in the late 18th century, by Paul and Thomas Sandby.

FACING PAGE TOP: Christopher Wren's proposals for remodelling the south front of the castle, never carried out because of the early death of King William III.

FACING PAGE CENTRE: Plan of the garden designed for Queen Anne by Henry Wise in 1712. The aerial photograph below of the area between the North Terrace and the Thames was taken by the Royal Air Force in 1964. This clearly shows traces of Henry Wise's garden exactly following the design of the plan.

The Hanoverians

Despite the concessions which the hill-top citadel could now offer towards the comforts of a country house it held few attractions for Queen Anne's Hanoverian successors, who vastly preferred the elegant apartments provided by Wren for King William III in the riverside palace of Hampton Court. Royal visits to Windsor were reduced to the occasional gathering of the Knights of the Garter. Once more the monarch's apartments were neglected, and fell into disrepair, while much of the other accommodation was made over to tenants.

This was the state of the castle when King George III, the first sovereign of the House of Hanover to be born in Britain and to speak English as his mother tongue, paid a visit to Windsor in 1776. By then the royal quarters were uninhabitable: but the 'neat little seat' opposite the south front which Queen Anne had preferred to the castle itself caught Queen Charlotte's eye, and the king made her a present of it. Their periodic occupation of 'Queen's Lodge', as it was now called, marked the start of an association with Windsor which lasted until the king's death 40 years later.

To house their still growing family of ten children the accommodation in the tiny lodge was soon supplemented by Nell Gwynn's house nearby. When this addition also proved inadequate the king instructed his architect and former drawing master, Sir William Chambers, to enlarge the lodge itself. The result was a dull building, so lacking in inspiration that some have attributed its design to the pupil rather than the master. But if the outside looked less like a palace than a barrack block, the interior nevertheless provided all the modest comforts needed by its inhabitants. This incongruous addition to the south aspect of the castle, stigmatized by Horace Walpole as 'plain even to meanness', was to stand for over 40 years.

A more permanent alteration to the surroundings of the castle was the filling in of the ditch which ran alongside the wall on all sides except the north. The removal of this medieval feature, dictated by sanitary reasons—private houses which then stood along its edge used to throw their refuse into it—took the castle one step further along the road from fortress to country house.

Meanwhile the larger rooms in the castle itself were in good enough condition to use for entertainment. On the Prince of Wales's birthday in 1780, for example, they provided the setting for a concert, followed by a ball, and open house was kept all day both at the castle and at Queen's Lodge, no one who applied being turned away without a glass of wine or ale and a slice of cake. The friendly attitude and open hospitality of the monarch did not, however, diminish the need for suitable decorum in the presence of royalty. Sentries were instructed not to permit servants or boys to 'gallop about the court', to exclude from the castle 'higglers of meat, fish or greens', and to prevent articles from being cried out for sale.

The king grew to love Windsor above all his other residences. Here this kindly and unpretentious monarch could live as a country squire, mixing informally with the townspeople on his terrace, clad in the simple suiting which came to be known as the 'Windsor Uniform', and which the Royal Family still use at Windsor in the evenings. He could also look after his farms, in which he maintained an active interest.

ABOVE: King George I. Medal by John Croker commemorating his arrival in Britain, 1714.

50

ABOVE: The south-east corner of the castle in the time of King George III, by Paul Sandby. The rooms in the south-east tower were used by his eldest son, the future King George IV.

RIGHT: Queen's Lodge, the house lived in by King George III for over 20 years, while the castle was being repaired. The king, Queen Charlotte and some of the princesses are shown walking on the South Terrace of the castle.

His experiments in methods of husbandry developed in Norfolk and Flanders led to the formation in the Great Park of two farms, still known as the Norfolk and Flemish farms, while the Merino sheep of Australia and New Zealand are largely descended from a flock bred by him at Windsor, partly from animals smuggled out of Spain.

The enlarged Queen's Lodge was never intended as more than a *pied-à-terre*, and as the king's attachment to Windsor grew, so he became increasingly resolved to bring the old royal apartments back into use. This called for a massive programme of repair and reconstruction, which started with the rooms on the south front nearest to the lodge, first used as royal apartments by King James II before his accession to the throne. The tower at the south-east corner was fitted up for the Prince of Wales—an arrangement which was eventually to have a decisive effect on the future layout of the sovereign's private apartments—while neighbouring suites were prepared for his brothers of York and Clarence. Some years afterwards another set of rooms was arranged on the east front for Queen Charlotte, and yet others for various of the princesses and princes. For himself the king fitted up a range of rooms on the gloomy ground floor overlooking the North Terrace, underneath the old apartments of King Charles II, which he had reserved for entertainment and ceremonial purposes. King Charles's rooms were to be purged of their Baroque extravagances, which he thought unsuitable for a medieval fortress, and converted into a Gothic palace. The architect chosen for the work, James Wyatt, started by restoring a Gothic shape to the numerous windows. This considerable task was never completed, and the still greater one of fully Gothicizing the interior hardly progressed further than the staircase. But all the rooms were restored and made habitable, and the full reoccupation of the royal apartments was celebrated by a great housewarming party in 1805. Unhappily the person most intimately affected by these sweeping and costly changes was the least satisfied: Queen Charlotte confessed to a friend that she had moved from a 'very comfortable and warm habitation' to 'the coldest house, rooms and passages that ever existed'.

Whatever the comforts of the new lodgings, they were well provided with works of art. From the beginning of his long reign the king had made substantial additions to the Royal Collection, starting with his purchase of the great collection formed by the British Consul in Venice, Joseph Smith, which contained among other things a splendid range of paintings and drawings by Canaletto. Following the example set by King Charles II, King George brought many paintings to Windsor, including great canvases by Rubens and Van Dyck which are still in the castle today. He had inherited some of the finest of these from his father, Frederick, Prince of Wales, a discerning collector, who but for his premature death would have come to the throne in 1760.

Having been afflicted all his life from the effects of a rare disease diagnosed today as porphyria, which led to recurrent bouts of delirium, the king suffered the permanent loss of his reason only five years after his reoccupation of the castle. Already over 70, he was to spend his last ten years a virtual prisoner in the lonely ground floor suite which he had furnished for himself at the opposite end of the royal apartments from those of the rest of his family. He died in 1820, and was buried in a large vault under what is now the Albert Memorial Chapel, excavated on his instructions some years earlier to form a tomb for himself and his family.

The improvements he had made to the castle, extensive though they

FACING PAGE ABOVE: Westminster Bridge, with Westminster Hall and Westminster Abbey behind, and a procession of barges and sailing boats moving upstream, 1746–7. One of 143 drawings by Canaletto in the collection of Joseph Smith, British Consul in Venice, bought by King George III in 1762.

FACING PAGE BELOW: The Bacino di S. Marco in Venice on Ascension Day, with the Bucintoro at the Molo. The Doge is on board, having returned from the mouth of the Lido, where he has cast a ring into the sea as a symbol of the union between Venice and the Adriatic, a ceremony commemorating the naval victory over the Dalmatians at the end of the 10th century. One of the 50 oil paintings by Canaletto in the collection of Joseph Smith bought by King George III in 1762.

53

ABOVE: The south-east corner of the castle after its reconstruction by Wyatville for King George IV. This watercolour by Joseph Nash shows a military review in progress in the 1840s, in the presence of Queen Victoria.

BELOW: The east front of the castle after its reconstruction by Wyatville, showing the formal garden. The group on the east terrace towards the left, above and behind the formation of soldiers, includes the young Queen Victoria and Prince Albert.

FACING PAGE ABOVE: The Long Walk today, showing the extension of the carriage-way up to the castle, made by King George IV, and the gateway named after him giving access to the Quadrangle beyond.

Here The Duke of Edinburgh, as President of the Fédération Equestre Internationale, leads the procession of competitors in the World Four-in-Hand Carriage Driving Championships to Smith's Lawn, Windsor Great Park, for the opening ceremony in September 1980, accompanied by his coachman, D. Saunders. The horses are, on the left, Harrier, a mare bred by The Queen by a Cleveland Bay stallion out of an Oldenburg mare and, on the right, Frederick, a Danish gelding.

FACING PAGE BELOW: The south-east corner of the castle today.

were, did not begin to satisfy the more grandiose ideas of his son and successor, King George IV. Having lost the forbidding majesty of a fortress at the hands of King Charles II, the rugged stone walls of this ancient stronghold could still never fully attain the relaxed charm of the country house, while the rooms remained cramped and draughty. Some other solution was required, which would combine the imposing character of a medieval castle with the comforts to be expected of a great house in the 19th century. After spending two months in the confined apartments on the south-east corner which he had occupied as Prince of Wales nearly 30 years earlier, the king called on his artistic adviser, Sir Charles Long, to make suggestions. The most radical of Long's proposals were carried out to the letter. The design of the exterior was to revert as far as possible to the architecture of the time of King Edward III, but with picturesque rather than dungeon-like features, including generous windows for comfort, and fanciful towers and battlements for romance. To give a focus to the whole the squat and unimpressive Round Tower of King Henry II was to be doubled in height, and given its quota of battlements. The carriageway of the Long Walk, which King Charles II had been unable to bring right up to the south front because of private houses which stood in its path, was to be completed, and carried directly into the quadrangle under a grand new gateway pierced through the south wall. This arrangement entailed the demolition of Queen's Lodge, which also stood in the way. As to the interior, all the rooms on the south and east fronts, including those occupied by the king, were to be linked by a new connecting corridor running along two of the inner sides of the quadrangle.

The architect chosen for this work was Jeffry Wyatt, soon, with the king's permission, to be renamed Wyatville, an appellation which he presumably thought more imposing. 'Veal or mutton', quipped His Majesty, 'call yourself what you like.' As reconstruction proceeded most of the timbers in the Upper Ward were found to be rotten, and few rooms escaped total renovation. The sovereign's private apartments, which had been sited for 600 years on the north front, were now moved to the south-east corner, where the king had lived as Prince of Wales, and the earlier apartments converted into a suite for the entertainment of visitors of state, and for other ceremonial purposes. An open courtyard within the earlier block was transformed into a picture gallery, known as the Waterloo Chamber, for the display of the series of portraits by Sir Thomas Lawrence of sovereigns, commanders and statesmen who had contributed to the downfall of Napoleon. The smaller rooms on the east front, now linked by the new corridor, were joined up to make large saloons for private entertainment, while others on the south front were converted for the use of guests. So well planned and executed was this work that nothing in the way of major reconstruction has been needed since.

It was this king who finally solved the problem of the garden, which had so concerned King Edward VI three centuries earlier. He made it possible to create a formal garden on the exposed ground outside the east front by enclosing it within a tall stone bastion, whose top was level with, and provided a prolongation of, the terraces. This gave it the appearance of a sunken garden, while affording protection from the searching winds which scour the top of the hill. So confident was Wyatville of the efficacy of this arrangement that he planned it as an orange garden, with an orangery under the northern bastion to house the trees in winter.

ABOVE: King George IV when Prince Regent, dressed in armour. Detail from a drawing in chalk on canvas by Sir Thomas Lawrence, 1814.

FACING PAGE: The Grand Reception Room. Formerly the King's Guard Chamber, this room was remodelled for King George IV by Wyatville in the style of Louis XV as a place of assembly for guests invited to functions in the adjoining Waterloo Chamber (page 60). Its handsome gilt plasterwork includes clusters of musical instruments over the doors, and groups of cherubs making music and dancing.

The decoration of the room is designed around a series of six tapestries made in the Gobelins factory in the 18th century, and bought for the king in 1825. Based on paintings by J. F. de Troy, they depict the story of Jason and the Golden Fleece.

The furniture, some of which came from Carlton House, the king's former residence in London, is covered with Beauvais tapestry of the same period. The large malachite vase was presented to Queen Victoria by the Emperor Nicholas I of Russia in 1844.

If King George IV's buildings were on the grand scale so were his purchases of works of art. The French Revolution and the subsequent invasion by French armies of the Low Countries had placed magnificent pictures, sculptures, furniture, tapestry and porcelain on the international market, and he bought them in quantity. Nor, as we have seen, did he neglect English artists. Besides the famous series of portraits by Lawrence in the Waterloo Chamber, many other masterpieces acquired or commissioned by this discerning collector are to be seen at Windsor.

It is a sad reflection that the monarch who carried out the greatest and most lavish reconstruction of the castle, and to whom its present appearance is largely due, should scarcely have survived to enjoy it himself. His new apartments were only ready for occupation towards the end of 1828, and he took up residence early in December. He moved out again the following April to allow further improvements to be made, paying frequent visits to check progress, and coming back into residence shortly before Christmas. Once more he remained until the following April but while still in the castle he fell ill, and he died in June. By then the central feature of his remodelled State Apartments, the Waterloo Chamber, was still unfinished, so that he was never able to see Lawrence's portraits in their intended setting.

But if his own enjoyment of the renovated castle was short, his successors made full use of it. The day after his funeral his brother King William IV made a tour of inspection, and soon moved in with all his family. There was not much left for the new king to do, beyond finishing off the works started by his brother: but he provided one facility which the castle had hitherto lacked—a library. For this he converted a series of rooms at the far end of the old State Apartments, including Queen Elizabeth's Gallery and the adjacent tower built by her grandfather, King Henry VII. This was the last major constructional work in the interior of the Upper Ward.

ABOVE LEFT: Sir Jeffry Wyatville, by Sir Thomas Lawrence. Wyatville carried out the last great reconstruction of the castle for King George IV. Before the architect is a plan of the Round Tower, whose height he raised by 30 feet. The picture was commissioned by King George IV.

FACING PAGE: The Duke of Wellington, by Sir Thomas Lawrence. One of the series of portraits by this artist of personages who played a part in the defeat of Napoleon which was assembled by King George IV and hangs in the Waterloo Chamber.

In his right hand the duke holds the Sword of State, which he had carried at a thanksgiving service in St Paul's Cathedral (shown in the background) the year before. Near its hilt lies his baton, beside the letter in which the king (then Prince Regent) signified his promotion to the rank of Field Marshal.

The Waterloo Chamber, created by King George IV to commemorate the victory of Waterloo.

While still Prince Regent the future king had commissioned Sir Thomas Lawrence to paint the portraits of all those who had played a prominent part in the resistance to Napoleon. As part of the reconstruction of the castle after his accession he instructed his architect, Wyatville, to use an open courtyard in the middle of the former apartments of King Charles II for a new gallery where they could be displayed. He did not live to see the result.

The panels of wood carving by Grinling Gibbons and his associates on the walls and balcony were moved from other rooms in the State Apartments. The fretwork on the upper section of the walls was added in the reign of Queen Victoria.

Here we see the north wall of the gallery, with the portrait of King George III, still alive in 1815 but having sadly lost his reason, in the central position over the fireplace. On his left is his son and successor King George IV, then Prince Regent, and on his right King William IV, in whose reign the gallery was completed. The portrait of King William, who came to the throne after Lawrence's death, is by David Wilkie. On King William's right is Robert, Earl of Liverpool, Prime Minister in 1815, and on King George IV's left is Robert, Viscount Castlereagh, Foreign Secretary. The room is dominated by the portrait of the Duke of Wellington (over the balcony) with that of the Russian commander Count Platoff, Hetman of the Cossacks, to the left.

The table, which seats over 80 persons, is laid for the luncheon which The Queen gives for the Knights of the Garter at their periodic gatherings. It is also used for many other functions and entertainments, such as concerts, plays, balls, and other large gatherings. The carpet, made in Agra, is said to be the largest seamless carpet ever made.

ABOVE: Pope Pius VII by Sir Thomas Lawrence.

One of the finest in the series commissioned by King George IV to commemorate the downfall of Napoleon, and now hung in the Waterloo Chamber (page 60). Painted in Rome in 1819.

RIGHT: One of a pair of Sèvres porcelain vases, with two gilt bronze handles, each in the form of a goat. Originally the property of Louis XVI, the vases were bought by King George IV in 1812.

FACING PAGE: King George IV by Sir Thomas Lawrence.

In this portrait, which hangs in St James's Palace, the king wears his coronation robes. His hand rests on the *Table des Grands Capitaines*, a circular table made for, but never delivered to, Napoleon, bearing portraits of famous military commanders of antiquity. On this table rests his imperial crown.

The painting of the king which hangs in the Waterloo Chamber (page 60) is a version of the same portrait, showing him in robes of the Order of the Garter.

63

ABOVE: Cabinet in veneered woods bearing plaques of Sèvres porcelain with mounts of chased gilt bronze by Martin Carlin. Bought by King George IV.

LEFT: One of a pair of corner cupboards in red and black lacquer with gilt bronze mounts by Bernard II van Risemburgh. It was bought by King George IV. Standing on the cupboard is a 15th-century Chinese celadon vase with French mounts.

RIGHT: Marble bust of King George II by Roubiliac. Presented to King George IV when Prince Regent.

RIGHT: The actor David Garrick and his wife, by William Hogarth. Garrick, engaged in the composition of an epilogue, is about to be interrupted by his wife. In 1777 Garrick was summoned to give a reading at Windsor, which to the delight of the royal children included imitations of bird noises. The picture was bought by King George IV.

BELOW: King George III returning from hunting through Eton, with Windsor Castle in the background, by Thomas Rowlandson. Acquired by King George IV, the first English sovereign to form a collection of English drawings.

The King's State Bedchamber.

The name of this room derives from its function in the apartments of King Charles II. It was not where he actually slept, because in earlier centuries the State Bedchamber, to which only trusted friends and advisers of the monarch were admitted, had become the place in which the more secret affairs of state were discussed and settled, like the Cabinet Room of today. As monarchs came to prefer more privacy, so they chose to sleep elsewhere than in their place of business. The state bed remained, but lacked an occupant.

The present appearance of the room no longer reflects this function, because it was remodelled during King George IV's reconstruction to form a bedroom in fact as well as in name. It was transformed into one of the two bedrooms in a suite designed for the reception of foreign sovereigns.

The bed, probably by the French cabinet maker Georges Jacob, was placed here by Queen Victoria for the state visit of Napoleon III and the Empress Eugénie in 1855. The hangings of purple and green are in the Napoleonic colours, and bear the embroidered monograms LN EI (Louis Napoleon, Eugénie Imperatores) at the foot.

The pictures hanging in this room when the photograph was taken include Gainsborough's portrait of the oboist Johann Christian Fischer (to right of bed), the Piazzetta in Venice looking towards the church of S. Maria della Salute by Canaletto, and Francis, 1st Marquess of Hastings by Sir Joshua Reynolds.

The Aubusson carpet was presented to The Queen by President de Gaulle in 1960.

ABOVE: The King's Drawing Room.
Originally known as the King's Withdrawing Room – a private room to which the king would withdraw either from his Audience Chamber or from his Dining Room, both of which lay next door – this room was remodelled by King George IV to form the principal drawing room in the suite which he created for visiting sovereigns. The pictures are by Rubens and his school.

LEFT: St Martin dividing his cloak, painted by Van Dyck in 1620, when he was much under the influence of Rubens, and now hanging in the King's Drawing Room.

FACING PAGE: The Queen's Drawing Room.
This performed the same function for Queen Catherine of Braganza as the King's Drawing Room did for the king. It is now hung with paintings of the early Stuart period.

FACING PAGE ABOVE: The Queen's Guard Chamber. No visitor could reach the Audience Chamber of the king or queen without passing their guard. This was the guard chamber of Queen Catherine of Braganza. Much enlarged in King George IV's reconstruction, it is used for the display of military relics.

FACING PAGE BELOW: The Garter Throne Room. Used by King Charles II as his Presence and Audience Chambers (the arch marks the division), this room was converted in the reign of King George IV to form a place of assembly for the Knights of the Garter. It is here that the sovereign invests new Knights with their robes and insignia. The State Portrait of The Queen hangs above the fireplace (see page 87).

ABOVE: The Queen's Ball Room, which served Queen Catherine of Braganza as the principal ball room of the castle. Since King George IV's reconstruction that function has usually been fulfilled by one of the larger rooms in the State Apartments, but it is still on occasions put to its original purpose. The crystal chandeliers were commissioned by King George III.

Although heavily foreshortened
(compare the illustration on page
11), this unusual aerial view shows
the east front of the castle with
remarkable clarity. The massive
windows of the Private Apartments
constructed by King George IV
overlook his formal garden, whose
layout was redesigned during the
present reign. On the right,
underneath the terrace, stands the
Orangery, now housing a swimming-
pool. Still on the right, behind the
east front, are the State Apartments,
with the high roof-line of the
Waterloo Chamber in the middle.
To the left, beyond the Round
Tower, lie St George's Chapel and
the Lower Ward.

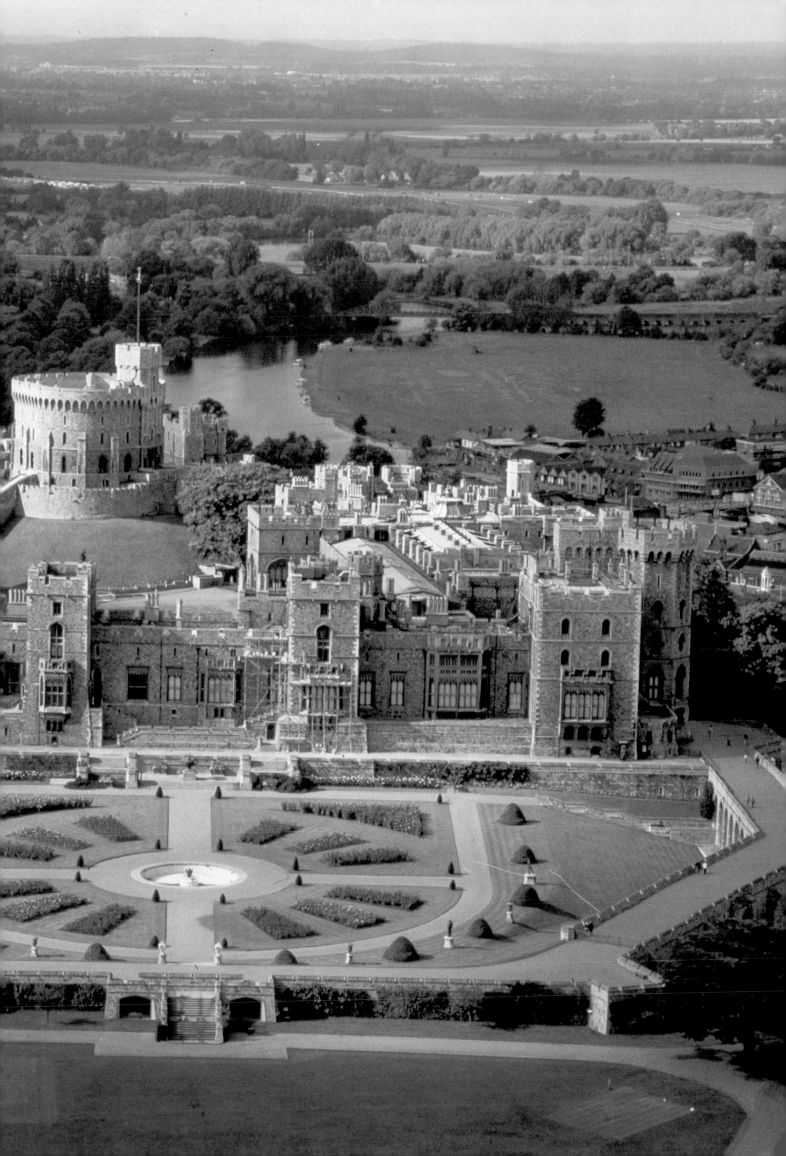

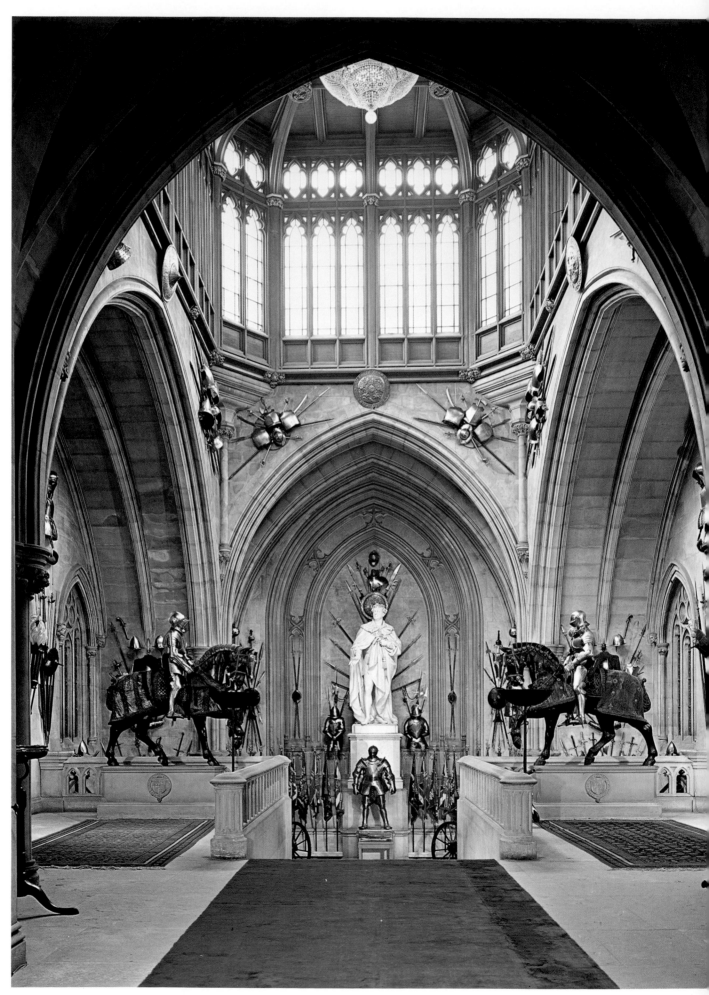

Queen Victoria

When Queen Victoria came to the throne in 1837 Windsor was still the best part of a day's journey from London, and offered the pleasures of a quiet country retreat away from the bustle of town. With the coming of the railways in the middle of the century distances shrank. Ministers could travel from London and back in a day, and the castle came increasingly to be used at times when government business was heavy. The splendid ceremonial rooms created by King George IV in the State Apartments were the setting for a series of state visits, the success of which afforded ample justification for the grand ideas which had inspired their design, as well as for the colossal expense of turning those ideas into reality. But for relaxation the queen must now look to more distant parts. With her husband, Prince Albert, later accorded the title of Prince Consort, she chose two properties at opposite extremities of the kingdom, Osborne in the Isle of Wight and Balmoral in the Highlands of Scotland, which happened to come on the market. As communications improved these two delightful estates increasingly supplanted Windsor as holiday homes.

It was at Windsor that the Prince Consort died in 1861 at the early age of 42. The queen, plunged into inconsolable grief, withdrew from public life for many years, and rarely set foot in London. She spent as long as she could each year in Osborne and Balmoral, and it was Windsor's turn to supplant Buckingham Palace as her normal residence when she had to be near the capital. With the passage of time she gradually emerged from her solitude, and although still shrinking from public contacts she entertained increasingly at home. Feeling unable to attend concerts, plays or the opera in public, she arranged performances at Windsor for the amusement of her guests and family, reviving a practice started in her husband's lifetime. When she emerged from her seclusion to celebrate her Golden Jubilee in 1887 the rapturous ovation which the surprised queen received from her subjects was marked at Windsor by a great gathering of her continental relations, including many future crowned heads. Kipling's 'widow at Windsor' had become the 'grandmother of Europe'.

When the old queen died in 1901 she was buried beside her husband within the remarkable mausoleum which she had built for him at Frogmore, in the private grounds of the castle.

ABOVE: Prince Albert, by F. X. Winterhalter.

LEFT: Queen Victoria and Prince Albert riding through George IV Gate.

FACING PAGE: The Grand Staircase. This staircase, designed by Anthony Salvin in 1866, was Queen Victoria's principal contribution to the State Apartments. It stands on the site of one of the open courtyards, medieval in origin, around which the apartments of King Charles II were constructed, dominated by the huge marble statue by Sir Francis Chantrey of King George IV, to whose taste and initiative the present appearance of the castle is largely due.

ABOVE: Watercolour drawing of St George's Hall after its reconstruction by Wyatville, painted by Joseph Nash. The table is set for a banquet given in 1844 to King Louis-Philippe of the French, who is shown entering the room with Queen Victoria.

RIGHT: The angle of the Grand Corridor constructed by Wyatville for King George IV in order to link the rooms of his new private apartments. Watercolour by Joseph Nash, 1846.

FACING PAGE: Queen Victoria in the robes of the Order of the Garter, by F. X. Winterhalter. This portrait hangs in the Garter Throne Room (page 70).

ABOVE: Queen Victoria invests King Louis-Philippe of France with the insignia of the Order of the Garter in the Garter Throne Room (for the appearance of this room today see page 70). Watercolour by Louis Haghe.

LEFT: Queen Victoria conducts Napoleon III, Emperor of the French, into the State Apartments. The Lord Chamberlain and the Lord Steward walk backwards before the royal party, holding their wands of office. Watercolour by G. Thomas, 1855.

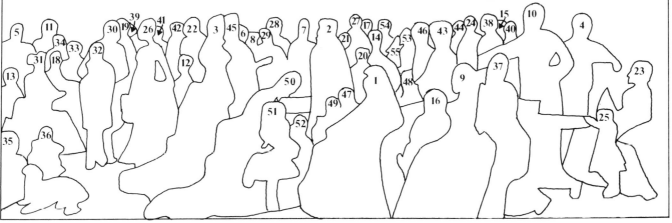

Queen Victoria surrounded by her
family in the Green Drawing Room
of the castle in 1887, the year of her
Golden Jubilee. The painting is by
Laurits Tuxen.

ABOVE: The Horseshoe Cloister, built in about 1480, when the choir of St George's Chapel was still under construction, as quarters for the priest-vicars or lesser clergy. It now houses the lay clerks, or men singers in the chapel choir. It owes its present appearance to a thorough restoration by George Gilbert Scott in 1870. Behind it rises the pointed roof of the Curfew Tower, added in 1863 to the original 13th-century structure, which contains the dungeon illustrated on page 13 and which is open to visitors.

LEFT: The west front of St George's Chapel. According to Queen Victoria the great west door was first used in 1871, at the wedding of her fourth daughter, Princess Louise. The steps proved so inadequate that they were replaced in the following year. It is now in regular use on great ceremonial occasions, such as the annual service of the Order of the Garter. Here The Queen and the Duke of Edinburgh leave the chapel by carriage after the service, watched by the Queen Mother, the Prince of Wales and the Knights Companion.

FACING PAGE: The richly decorated interior of the Albert Memorial Chapel was created by George Gilbert Scott for Queen Victoria in 1863–73 to commemorate her husband, Albert, the Prince Consort, who died in 1861 at the early age

of 42. The exterior of the building chosen to house it, originally the Lady Chapel for St George's Chapel, is illustrated on page 18.

In the centre of the foreground stands a cenotaph by H. de Triqueti in memory of the Prince, whose tomb is in the Royal Mausoleum at Frogmore. The illustrated panels around the walls, depicting scenes from Scripture, were also designed by Triqueti. Executed in a technique known as Tarsia, each design is incised on a marble panel, and the incisions are then filled with powdered marble of different colours. Above each panel is a sculptured head by Susan Durant portraying one of Queen Victoria's children. The vaulted ceiling is decorated in Venetian glass mosaic by Antonio Salviati. The figures in the false west window, also by Salviati, represent sovereigns, ecclesiastics and others closely connected with the castle.

The chapel also serves as a place of burial for two of Queen Victoria's descendants whose deaths were even more premature than that of the Prince Consort. The elaborate bronze structure in the centre, by Alfred Gilbert, forms the tomb of her grandson Albert-Victor, Duke of Clarence, who would have succeeded to the throne if he had survived his father, King Edward VII, but he died in 1892 at the age of 28. Concealed behind it lies the marble tomb, by J. Boehm, of her fourth son, Prince Leopold, Duke of Albany, who died in 1884 at the age of 30.

ABOVE: Four generations of sovereigns. Queen Victoria holds on her lap her great-grandson, the future King Edward VIII, later Duke of Windsor, born in 1894. Behind her stand her eldest son, later King Edward VII (right), and his son, later King George V.

ABOVE: The Royal Mausoleum at Frogmore by H. W. Brewer. This watercolour, painted in 1869, shows the interior soon after its completion. The remains of Prince Albert, who died in 1861, had recently been interred in the central tomb, to be joined by those of the queen over 30 years later in 1901.

The interior of the mausoleum was designed by Professor Ludwig Gruner of Dresden, Prince Albert's artistic adviser, to reflect the genius of Raphael, whom the prince regarded as the greatest artist of all time. Each one of the many paintings and sculptures commissioned for it followed some composition of the Master.

RIGHT: This photograph, taken in 1895, shows Queen Victoria with her youngest daughter, Princess Beatrice, in her private sitting room in the castle.

King Edward VII

With the accession of King Edward VII the castle sprang to life once more. Its new owner, the most gregarious of monarchs, was never happy except in company. After a pause for the installation of new-fangled creature comforts such as bathrooms and electric light, and some rearrangement of furnishings and works of art, the state and private apartments witnessed a succession of glittering functions which surpassed anything in the heyday of Queen Victoria's reign. Foreign sovereigns were once more entertained as visitors of state, guests filled the house for Ascot races, and Knights of the Garter assembled in their colourful robes for the investiture of new members of the order. For the formal reception of ministers and ambassadors a new audience chamber was created, ornamented with a dazzling array of Renaissance gems and jewels, most of which formed part of the collection acquired from Consul Smith of Venice by King George III at the beginning of his reign. The apartments which his son, King George IV, had fashioned but never lived to enjoy thus finally came into their own.

The nine years of King Edward's brief reign brought not only the castle, but also the very workings of the monarchy, back to life. No longer was the head of state a remote figure, preoccupied by personal sorrows, to be approached with awe and addressed with infinite tact. In the presence of the new sovereign statecraft went hand in hand with relaxation. Monarchs, statesmen and envoys could forgather on terms of easy familiarity under their genial host and probe each others' minds. After his death in 1910 his son, King George V, followed his hospitable example. It was, for instance, nothing out of the ordinary that the Ascot house party of 1914 should have included the ambassadors of Austria and Russia, two major powers who were to find themselves on opposite sides in the First World War.

ABOVE: King Edward VII by Sir Luke Fildes. Study from the life for the State Portrait.

84

The House of Windsor

One consequence of the ensuing hostilities was an event which bound the king and his family even closer to the oldest of their homes. The tensions of war made it necessary to find a new name for the dynasty. Since the accession of King Edward this had been known as the House of Saxe-Coburg-Gotha, the German princely family to which the Prince Consort had belonged. In 1917 it was changed, by a happy inspiration, to the House of Windsor.

After a break for the duration of the war, the return of peace brought a revival of royal hospitality. In this the king found support from his consort, Queen Mary, not only as hostess but also in setting the scene for indoor entertainment. Her experience as a collector, strengthened by an encyclopaedic knowledge of European royal families, led to a close interest in the interior of each palace and its contents. Few royal owners have known them so intimately. She inspired many catalogues, notes in her hand about individual pieces abound, and parts of the interior of the castle still bear the imprint of her taste.

The death of her husband in 1936 led to the accession, and abdication within the year, of King Edward VIII. The new king spent little time in the castle, preferring the less formal atmosphere of Fort Belvedere, the small house centred around an 18th-century tower close to the southern border of the Great Park, where he had lived for six years as Prince of Wales. He left an enduring monument in the park in the shape of Smith's Lawn, the area where polo is now played. It was he who first had it levelled, not for polo but to form a small aerodrome.

Though he did not live within its walls it was from the castle that he broadcast his message of abdication before leaving the kingdom. But if it witnessed his final act of separation from throne and country it also provided a new link. The first act of his brother and successor, King George VI, on ascending the throne was to confer on him the title of Duke of Windsor.

King George VI possessed a house of his own near the castle—Royal Lodge, in the centre of the Great Park. However much he may have preferred its seclusion and more modest dimensions, unforeseen reasons soon made the ancient fortress indispensable to his family. Once more the clouds of war were gathering, and less than three years were to pass before the storm broke. With the fall of France in 1940 London was exposed to attack from the air. The castle was no further from the French coast than the capital, but it was less likely to attract strategic bombing, and its massive masonry offered some degree of protection against the lone raider. The king accordingly sent his daughters, Princess Elizabeth and Princess Margaret, then aged 14 and 9, to spend the rest of the war under its protection. Their parents joined them at Windsor for weekends, but spent the working week at Buckingham Palace. The wisdom of sending the princesses out of town was apparent when a stick of bombs fell on the palace itself. Both their Majesties were inside at the time, and considerable damage was done, but happily no one was hurt.

The later years of the princesses' stay at Windsor were marked by a series of pantomimes, performed in the Waterloo Chamber at successive Christmases, in which both Their Royal Highnesses took a leading

George V 1910–1936
Edward VIII 1936
George VI 1936–1952
Elizabeth II ....1952 whom
God preserve

FACING PAGE, ABOVE: The gathering of nine kings in the castle at the funeral of King Edward VII on 20 May 1910. From left to right, standing: King Haakon VII of Norway, King Ferdinand of Bulgaria, King Manoel of Portugal, the Emperor William II of Germany, King George I of the Hellenes, King Albert of the Belgians; sitting: King Alfonso of Spain, King George V, King Frederick VIII of Denmark.

FACING PAGE, BELOW LEFT: Queen Mary, by W. M. Rankin.

FACING PAGE, BELOW RIGHT: Head study of King George V by Kathleen Scott.

ABOVE: The State Portraits of King George VI and Queen Elizabeth by Sir Gerald Kelly.

The setting for these portraits is taken from a miniature construction devised by the architect Sir Edwin Lutyens as a reminiscence of Viceregal Lodge in Delhi. The artist received the commission for these paintings in 1938, moved the canvases to Windsor on the outbreak of war, and did not complete them until 1945.

LEFT: The Princesses Elizabeth (now Queen Elizabeth II) and Margaret with Queen Elizabeth during a rehearsal in the Waterloo Chamber for one of the pantomimes performed at Christmas during the war years.

FACING PAGE: The State Portrait of Her Majesty Queen Elizabeth II by James Gunn.

role, to the delight of all present. The celebrated series of paintings by Lawrence which lined the walls in peacetime had been sent away for safety, and their place was taken by portraits of leading pantomime characters such as Dick Whittington, Puss in Boots and Jack and the Beanstalk. These light-hearted additions to the Royal Collection were not removed when Lawrence's august canvases were returned to their place, and remain to this day in position behind them. During the war many of the other works of art were sent away for safety, and it was some years after the return of peace before the castle returned to its normal splendour.

With the accession of Princess Elizabeth in 1952 as Her Majesty Queen Elizabeth II the castle became the home of a young and growing family for the first time since the early days of Queen Victoria's marriage. Over the years it has come to perform many functions: a weekend retreat where the Royal Family can engage in outdoor activities, such as riding, carriage driving, polo and shooting, and forgather in full strength at Christmas; a country house conveniently close to London where the Sovereign can offer hospitality to her ministers, to representatives of foreign and Commonwealth countries and to prominent citizens; and a setting for great ceremonial occasions such as visits of foreign heads of state, or the gatherings of the Knights of the Garter.

The hastily erected fortress of the Norman invaders has grown through the centuries into one of the most celebrated features of our national heritage. In no way an institutionalized museum, but a living royal home, parts of which can nevertheless be shared by the general public, its nine centuries of accumulated history fit it for the key role in the great pageantry of state which it so admirably fulfils.

Queen Mary's Dolls' House. This remarkable dolls' house was created for Queen Mary in 1921–4 to the design of the architect Sir Edwin Lutyens. An imaginary palace built to a scale of one-twelfth life size, it is fitted and decorated throughout in the finest materials, all its equipment functions, and its furniture and works of art differ only in size from their real counterparts. The list of its donors includes many prominent names, and a large number of leading manufacturers, craftsmen, artists and authors contributed to its contents.

ABOVE: The Library. Besides miniature printed books the Library includes many volumes containing original works by prominent authors and poets of the day, often in their own handwriting, and richly bound in gilt-tooled morocco. The cabinets contain a collection of over 700 miniature drawings and watercolours by well-known artists, as well as fifty volumes of music by contemporary British composers. The portrait of Queen Elizabeth I is by Sir William Nicholson, and that of Henry VIII by Sir Arthur Cope.

ABOVE LEFT: The Queen's Bathroom. The bath and basin are of alabaster with silver taps, the floor of mother-of-pearl, and the walls of green shagreen, with the dado and imposts of ivory. The ceiling is painted with mermaids. One of the lifts can be seen on the right of the lobby beyond the door.

ABOVE RIGHT: The Queen's Bedroom. The bed and walls are hung with silk damask. The overmantel of white marble and jade surrounds the portrait by Frank O. Salisbury of the Duchess of Teck, Queen Mary's mother.

LEFT: The Entrance Hall is paved in marble and lapis lazuli, and the fine staircase is in marble, with a wrought iron balustrade.

LEFT: Guard Mounting in the Quadrangle showing (left to right) King Edward III Tower, St George's Gate, Round Tower and the Grand Entrance to the State Apartments. The Guards are wearing Winter Order.

LEFT: The Guard Mounting ceremony, which takes place either in the Quadrangle or in Engine Court if the Court is in residence. During the summer months when the Court is not in residence, Guard Mounting takes place on the lawn on Castle Hill, and in winter on the parade ground outside the Guard Room near Henry VIII's Gate.

LEFT: A State Visit – the scene in the Quadrangle. The photograph shows the Rank Past of the Life Guards and the Blues and Royals.
Her Majesty can be seen standing on the dais at the top of the picture with the Visiting Head of State.

ABOVE: The Queen inspecting The Queen's Company, 1st Battalion Grenadier Guards. Her Majesty is accompanied by the Duke of Edinburgh, Colonel of the Regiment. The Regiment has its origins in the 'Royal Regiment of Guards' raised by Charles II in 1656 while in exile.

RIGHT: The Guard of Honour, performed by the Scots Guards with the Queen's Company Colour, the band of the regiment and the Corps and Drums of the battalion, is mounted in the centre of the Quadrangle on the occasion of a State Visit.

ABOVE: The procession of the Order of the Garter through the Lower Ward towards the West Door of St George's Chapel. The Knights Companion, in their robes of Garter blue and their plumed hats, are rounding the corner at the bottom of the picture.

Founded in 1348 by King Edward III (see page 16) the Most Noble Order of the Garter is the highest order of chivalry in England. The Knights Companion, 24 in number, are appointed by the sovereign from persons prominent in public life. They assemble from time to time at Windsor. New Knights are invested with their robes and insignia in the Garter Throne Room (see page 70) and all the Knights then process through the castle to St George's Chapel for their service, at which the new Knights are installed.

LEFT: The Queen and the Duke of Edinburgh, returning by carriage from St George's Chapel to the Upper Ward, pass through the gate of the Horseshoe Cloister.

LEFT: Queen Elizabeth the Queen Mother with the Prince of Wales on the steps at the West Front of St George's Chapel.

BELOW: The Queen and The Duke of Edinburgh returning by carriage to the Upper Ward. The Most Noble Order of the Garter is popularly thought to have originated at Windsor when King Edward III danced with the Countess of Salisbury. During the dance the Countess lost her blue garter. To silence the amusement of the other dancers, the King held up the garter and vowed that it would be advanced to 'high honour and estimation'.

ABOVE: The Royal Family are noted for their love of horses and their passion both for watching and competing in equestrian events. The Prince of Wales is a keen polo player. He is seen here enjoying this fiercely competitive sport at Smith's Lawn in Windsor Great Park.

LEFT: Her Majesty and the Duchess of York at the Royal Windsor Horse Show. The Show was founded in 1943 and takes place each year in May. Members of the Royal Family participate in the events with great enthusiasm.

ABOVE: The Duke of Edinburgh negotiates one of the obstacles at Virginia Water, Windsor Great Park, during the cross-country phase of the World Four-in-Hand Carriage Driving Championships.

RIGHT: The Outriders and carriages leaving Windsor Castle for the Royal Ascot procession, in which five open landaus drive up the course. The first carriage carries the Sovereign and the Master of the Horse; in the following landaus are members of the Royal Family and guests who have been invited to Windsor for race week.

LEFT: The Scottish State Coach. The undercarriage and lower half of the body originally formed part of a glass coach built for the Duchess of Teck, mother of Queen Mary, in 1830. It was subsequently altered to an open landau and in 1969 a completely new top was made for it, with large glass windows and transparent panels in the roof.

ACKNOWLEDGEMENTS

The illustrations of portraits and objects in the Royal Collection and the photographs of the State Apartments and Queen Mary's Dolls' House are from The Royal Collection, St James's Palace, Copyright Her Majesty The Queen.

The illustrations of the interior of St George's Chapel are reproduced by kind permission of the Dean and Canons.

The reconstructions of the castle in the Middle Ages on pages 6 and 8–9 are by Terry Ball of the Inspectorate of Ancient Monuments, Department of the Environment, with advice from Peter Curnow, also of the Inspectorate, and from Professor Allen Brown of King's College, London.

Other illustrations are acknowledged as follows: Andy Williams Photographic Library: p. 80 (below); Michael Holford Library: p. 7; Robert W. Cameron: pp. 10–11, 72–3; Gerald Newbery, FIIP, FRPS: pp. 13 (below), 15 (above and below), 18 (above), 19 (below left and right), 22 (below), 55 (below), 81, 90 (below); Eton College Library: p. 14 (below); Godfrey Argent: pp. 18 (below), 19 (above), 80 (above); Bodleian Library, Oxford: p. 20; A. F. Kersting, FIIP, FRPS: pp. 23, 96; the Warden and Fellows of All Souls College, Oxford: p. 48 (top); the National Trust, Anglesey Abbey: pp. 54 (above and below), 75 (below); Tim Graham: pp. 55 (above), 92–3, 94–5; Popperfoto: p. 82 (above right); Radio Times Hulton Picture Library: p. 86 (below); Photolink (Anthony Jones) 90-1. Pitkin Pictorials, photo by John Freeman: front cover.

The Queen's Presents & Royal Carriages

An Exhibition of The Queen's Presents & Royal Carriages is open to the public at the same times as Queen Mary's Dolls' House and the exhibition of drawings (see below). The exhibition contains many unique items of interest which have been given to Her Majesty and The Duke of Edinburgh from all over the world for the Silver Jubilee and throughout the Queen's reign. It is housed in a part of the buildings which form the Mews at Windsor.

The precincts of Windsor Castle are open to the public except on days when special royal functions are taking place.

The State Apartments are also open, except on Sundays in winter and at certain times of the year just before, during or just after official residences of The Queen. As a general rule they are closed for the second half of March, the whole of April, three weeks in June and two weeks over Christmas. In winter they are open from 10.30a.m. to 3p.m. and in summer from 10.30a.m. to 5p.m.

Also open to the public, and not subject to closure when her Majesty is in official residence, is a standing exhibition of master drawings by such artists as Holbein and Leonardo da Vinci. Full-size colour reproductions of many of the finest are available.

Queen Mary's Dolls' House and the exhibition of carriages are open at the same times as the exhibition of drawings.

Works of art in the Royal Collection not on view in the State Apartments, or in other royal palaces open to the public such as the Palace of Holyroodhouse, Hampton Court Palace or Kensington Palace, may be seen in the periodic exhibitions mounted in The Queen's Gallery at Buckingham Palace.

FRONT COVER: The Long Walk, Windsor Castle.

BACK COVER: The King's State Bedchamber (see page 67).

© R. Mackworth-Young & Pitkin Pictorials 1982.
Reprinted, revised 1988.
Reprinted 1992.

Pitkin Pictorials Ltd, Healey House, Dene Road, Andover SP10 2AA. Produced by Mandarin Offset. Printed and bound in Hong Kong.

ISBN (hardback) 0 85372 402 4
ISBN (paperback) 0 85372 338 9